Praise for *Helping Your Child with Language-Based Learning Disabilities*

"Daniel Franklin has written a truly remarkable book about children with language-based learning disabilities. His work contains not only clear descriptions of different problems faced by children and adolescents with learning problems, but also realistic strategies for addressing these problems. I was especially impressed with Franklin's understanding of and empathy for children who struggle with learning, as well as for their parents, teachers, and other professionals who work with them. I found Franklin to be skilled at presenting the importance of helping youngsters to become more independent without prematurely removing the support that they require to navigate life's challenges. This book will serve as a major resource for parents and professionals—to be read and reread."

—**Robert Brooks, PhD**, faculty at Harvard Medical School (part-time), and coauthor of *Raising Resilient Children* and *The Power of Resilience*

"Daniel Franklin, a respected educational therapist, has written a thoughtful and empathetic book translating his experience helping many boys and girls into a practical guide. His advice takes into consideration first and foremost the child's feelings and preferences, and works to bring parents and their struggling child onto the same plane. He understands and emphasizes the importance of early identification and intervention, that there are no magic bullets, and that practice and more practice pay off. Franklin emanates positivity and patience, stressing kindness to children who have been exposed to more than their share of shaming and corrective input from adults."

—**Sally E. Shaywitz, MD**, professor of learning develop~~ment~~ cofounder and codirector of ~~the Yale Center for~~ Creativity, and author of *Ov*

"Parents of children with special needs are on a journey they didn't ask to take. There are many books that provide an aerial photograph of this voyage. *Helping Your Child with Language-Based Learning Disabilities* stands head and shoulders above the rest by offering a road map, a compass, a walking stick, and some snacks along the way. Daniel Franklin's experience, wisdom, and sensitivity shine through on every page. He can lead a concerned parent from feeling that 'my child *is* a problem' to the profound understanding that 'my child *has* a problem—and I can help.'"

—**Richard D. Lavoie, MA, MEd**, author of *The Motivation Breakthrough* and *It's So Much Work to Be Your Friend*

"Children who struggle with language-related learning issues, and their families, face the daunting prospect of navigating an education system that is not aligned to their unique neurobiological profiles. In this gem of a book, Franklin arms parents with the knowledge and strategies they need to support and advocate for their unique child—not just in learning to read or calculate but in developing to their full potential as a whole and happy human being. There are no quick fixes or magic beans here—the information presented amounts to a practical, reliable, and sensitively written guide."

—**Mary Helen Immordino-Yang, PhD**, professor of education at the University of Southern California (USC) Rossier School of Education, associate professor of psychology at USC's Brain and Creativity Institute, and author of *Emotions, Learning, and the Brain*

"Daniel Franklin provides practical steps to help children with language-based learning disabilities succeed not only at school, but also at life. His helpful advice is accessible, clear, and instructive; at the same time, it is supportive and empathetic. This book is essential for parents who struggle with how best to equip their children with the skills they need to navigate educational challenges. Franklin also teaches parents how to foster positivity and confidence in their children."

> —**Judy Ho, PhD**, clinical psychologist; two-time board diplomate of the American Board of Professional Psychology and the National Board of Forensic Evaluators; tenured associate professor of psychology at Pepperdine University; and frequent expert psychologist on leading television networks, including CNN, CBS, and FOX

"This is a truly *human* book for parents overwhelmed by the world of experts, incomprehensible advice, and reports they don't understand. Franklin writes, 'Your relationship is more important than schoolwork.' Imagine! If parents learn nothing more than this, they will have learned the essence of how to help their struggling child. This comprehensive book is a marvel that will help struggling parents breathe a whole lot easier."

> —**Dorothy Ungerleider, MA**, board-certified educational therapist, founder of the Association of Educational Therapists, and author of *Reading, Writing, and Rage* and *Educational Therapy in Action*

"This book is an outstanding resource not only for parents of children with language-based learning difficulties, but also for parents more generally. Written in a highly accessible way, it provides a warm, positive, and encouraging approach for supporting children through strong relationships between parents and children, and between families and educators."

> —**Amanda Datnow, PhD**, professor of education at the University of California, San Diego

"Daniel Franklin's remarkable book offers parents a wealth of strategies they can use to support their struggling children. Franklin's suggestions are easy to implement, and create a common language for parents and professionals. His compassionate approach will inspire and empower families, and provide students with hope and optimism. This is a must-read for anyone helping a child navigate the challenges of school and life."

> —**Richard L. Goldman, MEd**, teacher, administrator, and college professor with over forty years' experience in language-based learning disabilities and educational consulting

"*Helping Your Child with Language-Based Learning Disabilities* is a great resource for parents and education professionals. Franklin provides the understanding (and tools) necessary for parents to more effectively meet the learning needs of their children. The other great accomplishment of this book is its focus on education as a means to an end—that a positive educational experience can help children grow into adults who are successful and who thrive in their life pursuits."

> —**Michael E. Spagna, PhD**, provost and vice president of academic affairs at California State University, Dominguez Hills

Helping Your Child *with* Language-Based Learning Disabilities

Strategies to Succeed in School & Life with Dyslexia, Dysgraphia, Dyscalculia, ADHD & Processing Disorders

DANIEL FRANKLIN, PhD

New Harbinger Publications, Inc.

Publisher's Note

This publication is designed to provide accurate and authoritative information in regard to the subject matter covered. It is sold with the understanding that the publisher is not engaged in rendering psychological, financial, legal, or other professional services. If expert assistance or counseling is needed, the services of a competent professional should be sought.

Distributed in Canada by Raincoast Books

Copyright © 2018 by Daniel Franklin
     New Harbinger Publications, Inc.
     5674 Shattuck Avenue
     Oakland, CA 94609
     www.newharbinger.com

Scarborough's reading rope, in chapter 6, is reprinted from HANDBOOK FOR RESEARCH IN EARLY LITERACY, Volume 1 by Susan B. Neuman and David K. Dickinson, copyright © 2003 by Susan B. Neuman and David K. Dickinson. Reprinted with permission of Guilford Publications.

Cover design by Amy Shoup

Acquired by Ryan Buresh; Edited by Marisa Solis

Library of Congress Cataloging-in-Publication Data on file

Printed in the United States of America

21 20 19

10 9 8 7 6 5 4 3 2

For students and families everywhere

Contents

Part III:
Succeeding at Life

Foreword

Learning, especially for children with language-based learning difficulties, depends upon the quality of the connection these children have with their parents and teachers. Daniel Franklin and I both struggled in the early years of our schooling. I was not a natural student and required good teachers to succeed. Unfortunately, when I was growing up, good teachers were the exception rather than the rule. I was confused as to whether I was smart or stupid, and it never occurred to me that the teacher made the difference. It was only many years later that I came to realize that I was an excellent student in those classes where I cared for the teacher and felt that he or she cared for me. "Unteachable" students have yet to find the right teacher, which is why we, as parents, have to become active collaborators and provide our children with the level of support they need to be successful in school and in life.

Children with language-based learning difficulties often suffer from secondary emotional problems such as deep feelings of frustration, anger, anxiety, sadness, and shame. They can begin to isolate themselves from their friends, lose interest in meaningful activities, and withdraw into video games and other technologies that distract them from their feelings, thereby compounding the problems. It is vital to make sure that these challenges are faced together as a family and to prevent our children from feeling alone, stupid, and destined to fail. We must also resist the pressure to turn our children's struggles into a referendum on the quality of our parenting. All learning depends on the brain's ability to adapt to and store new information. This process, called neuroplasticity, depends upon low levels of stress, secure attachment relationships, and an open and receptive state of mind. If children and parents are emotionally shut down because of anxiety and shame, very little learning can occur in either parent or child.

For those of you struggling to find a way to help a child with language-based learning difficulties, you have stumbled upon an oasis in a vast desert with this book. You will find Daniel to be a wise and experienced guide through the maze of conflicting opinions, well-meaning advice, and sometimes remarkably expensive "solutions" to your child's learning difficulties. Daniel has the right combination of training, experience, and compassion to lead you through our complicated and confusing educational systems. He has worked with children, teens, and young adults for more than thirty years, helping thousands of students during the course of his long career in education.

What sets Daniel apart from many others is his understanding that brains don't learn in isolation but are embedded in bodies, which are woven into families and communities. Daniel and I both study interpersonal neurobiology, which views the brain as a social organ and learning as the outcome of social interaction, especially for children. When we frame learning as a collaborative process, we provide new opportunities to improve educational outcomes for all children.

Daniel understands the many detrimental effects that school can have on children with language-based learning difficulties. His book offers proven school- and life-skills support strategies for children and parents that are based on the principles of the social neuroscience of learning, attachment-based teaching, and mindful parenting. His strategies will help you support your child in all areas of learning by optimizing attuned and positive social interactions, which is the way our brains have evolved to learn.

It is possible to positively affect both learning outcomes and a child's emotional life at the same time, but we must remember to value the uniqueness of each individual and resist the pressure to expect our children (and ourselves) to live up to the standards and timetables of whatever is considered "normal" on any particular day. Daniel's strategies will help you advocate more effectively for your child, offer the support your child needs to manage schoolwork, and understand how your own special bond with your child can spark his or her interest in learning.

Most important, Daniel reminds us that our primary job as parents is to treasure our children and prevent the challenges of schoolwork from damaging our relationships with them. He shows us that our relationships with our children do not have to be compromised in order for them to learn or manage the demands of school. Daniel has taken a challenging aspect of our lives and made it not only manageable but also positive. As parents, we are automatically positioned to be central collaborators in our children's education. With this book, you now have the resource you are seeking to help your child be successful at school and in life.

—Louis Cozolino, PhD
Professor of Psychology at Pepperdine Graduate School of Education and Psychology and author of *The Neuroscience of Psychotherapy* and *The Social Neuroscience of Education*

Introduction

There are two stories of my childhood: one I share frequently and one I haven't discussed much until now. The first story is easy to tell: it's about a boy who grew up in the open air of Cape Cod surrounded by family, a life filled with adventure, and a new experience around every corner. It sounds like, and in many ways was, a wonderful childhood.

The other story is much harder for me to share: it's about how school—and my inability to learn like my peers—almost crushed me. Because despite an otherwise wonderful childhood, I was very nearly broken by my struggles in the classroom and the overwhelming lack of understanding—and kindness—offered to me by teachers.

In the 1970s, when I was in elementary school, my parents took a very hands-off approach, common among parents at that time. It was in vogue to allow children to explore the world and learn on their own. This may have been a great approach for other kids, but, for a kid like me, it was a disaster. In retrospect, it would have been nice if my parents were more aware of my struggles at school and recognized that I was in need of comprehensive help, but it was a different time. Instead, I struggled through school and encountered significant learning and behavior challenges.

My progress was slow, but with time and effort I earned my bachelor's degree from Boston University. I then went on to teach at two schools designed to address the educational needs of children with language-based learning difficulties (LBLDs).

I later earned my master of education in reading, language, and learning disabilities from Harvard University Graduate School of Education. While there, I taught at the Harvard Reading Lab under the direct supervision of my mentor Jeanne Chall, author of the seminal *Stages of Reading Development*. Later, I earned my PhD in education at

UCLA, and I began my private practice as a one-on-one reading teacher, organizational coach, academic tutor, and educational therapist.

Today, as an educational consultant, I help parents identify why their children are struggling in school and what they can do about it. I now work with a team of committed educators. Together, we offer hundreds of students a wide array of school-support services, including educational consulting, tutoring, academic management, and one-on-one schooling.

Until now, I haven't told many people just how hard school was for me when I was growing up. It has taken me my whole life to feel confident enough to share this part of my life without shame: to be able to recount my profound struggles to learn the alphabet, to reveal that I didn't learn to read until I was eleven years old, and so much more. But I've come to realize that my story matters tremendously—because it is the story of so many children I meet, who, like me as a child, have an unbelievably difficult time learning to read, write, and perform well at school.

Though it's been quite a journey to get to this place of acceptance, it's clear to me now that my difficulties as a student have played a significant role in my work. What I once saw as a deficit, I now consider an asset: I understand, as few others do, the emotional impact that language-based learning difficulties can have on children and families. My experiences, both good and bad, offer a unique lens through which to view my students' struggles.

I can tell you this: If your child can survive his or her years at school, he or she will almost certainly prevail in the years that lie beyond. But to get through those school years, your child will rely on you for the love, support, and encouragement needed to not give up.

A Relationship-Based Approach

Countless children arrive at my office on the cusp of being expelled from school on academic grounds, or because they're so despondent that they simply refuse to go to school. My primary responsibility is to give these young people *hope* and provide the *support* they need to be successful. I understand how essential hope and support are, because they were the ingredients that allowed me to find success in the face of so much failure.

My personal experience has been central to my discovery of a better, *kinder* approach to helping a child with a language-based learning disability—one that recognizes the critical role of healthy relationships in fostering motivation and learning. Over and over again, I have witnessed patience, understanding, and gentle guidance achieve what pure remediation programs rarely can: transform struggling children into confident and accomplished learners. I will teach you how to incorporate just such an approach when you help your child.

My number-one goal in this book is to teach you that *the most productive way to promote social, emotional, and learning development in children is by enhancing the quality of their relationship with their parents, caretakers, and teachers* (Cozolino 2013, Immordino-Yang 2016, Pianta 2000, Siegel and Hartzell 2013). In other words, creating a healthy relationship with your child is the best way to help him or her become a successful learner.

The parents I meet in my practice frequently describe feeling torn between their desire to help their children succeed and their desire to avoid "enabling." Too often, parents feel guilty providing homework and organization help because conventional thinking suggests that children should be able to perform these tasks independently. On the other hand, parents also feel guilty about not helping their children when they are suffering. (Though "suffering" may sound extreme, I can tell you from my own life and the lives of the children with whom I have worked that struggling in school is nothing if not extremely painful.) As a parent of a child with LBLDs, you likely have felt such conflict.

Throughout this book, I demonstrate that you, as a parent, are actually the greatest resource to alleviate your child's pain. Though their approach to my schooling was possibly too hands off, my parents nevertheless consistently expressed their unconditional love for me. Their unfailing belief that I was a worthy person—even if I wasn't a successful student—was, without a doubt, what allowed me to remain sufficiently motivated to not give up on school and myself. It was this level of motivation that helped me to survive my difficult school life and, eventually, thrive in a career that has allowed me to help children who struggle as I once did.

I have no doubt that if my parents had known how critical it is for parents to provide *both* unconditional love *and* high levels of academic assistance, they would have tried to be more involved in my schooling. Fortunately, our understanding of LBLDs has improved exponentially, as has our understanding of the most effective support techniques for children with these challenges. Now that we know better, we must do all we can to ensure that these children receive both the academic and emotional support they need to end the cycles of pain and frustration in which they are caught.

This book is my effort to do just that—to share how I help children with LBLDs succeed, by using the very type of support I wish had been more available to me. Through evidence and anecdotes, I will show you how kindness and collaboration really are the best ways to support your child. You will learn how to:

- Support your child when learning to read

- Support your child when expected to learn by reading

- Support your child when learning to write

- Help your child become an active learner through pre-teaching and preparation

- Engage your child in strategies for remembering and recalling important facts

- Become an effective organizational manager for your child's school materials and scheduling demands

- Become a compassionate cultivator of your child's ultimate independence

- Provide a high degree of assistance in a kind way

- Remain patient, thoughtful, and kind as you collaborate with your child

I've also provided a range of supplemental material available for download at the website for this book: http://www.newharbinger.com /40989. These extra checklists, tips, and resources will further enhance your ability to effectively support your child. (Refer to the very back of this book for more details on how to access the online materials.) By learning and practicing the strategies in this book, you absolutely can change your child's life!

No Quick Fixes

Supporting children with language-based learning difficulties often takes more time than expected. In a world of quick fixes, we are led to believe that children should be able to catch up to their grade level swiftly if they only work intensively enough, log enough hours on a computer program, or "try hard enough."

Many of the skills you may want your child to acquire can take months or even years to develop. Skills take a long time to develop because *brain development* takes a long time. In fact, the prefrontal cortex, which is responsible for virtually all of the capacities required for high-level learning and school success, is not fully formed until most people reach their twenties. That, along with the fact that each child develops skills on his or her own unique timetable, makes it impossible to know exactly when a particular skill will come on line. Furthermore, being a good student requires far more than just the acquisition of certain academic skills; doing well in school requires the development of an enormous number of coordinated skills across a broad range of capacities. Throughout this book, I will urge you to become comfortable with your child's unique developmental timeline. I will encourage you to pay greater attention to your child and yourself than to standards and societal expectations.

I understand why parents are nervous about long-term support. Many worry that their children may never develop all of the skills they need to get by in life. With my approach, your child will, for a time, come to depend on you to help manage the demands of school, learn content, acquire skills, and achieve success. But I will show you that this approach is actually the quickest means of fostering the independence we seek for all children.

The fastest route to a lifetime of dependence is withholding the support that is needed when it is needed. We must never put the objective of independence ahead of much more important things, such as skill development, learning, and healthy relationships with caregivers. With these come independence; it is not the other way around. It's also important not to expect immediate results. There are simply no "magic beans" to make your child grow faster, stronger, or more capable.

The kind of help I advocate requires a profound lifestyle shift for your whole family—*not* a set of quick fixes. Mine is a method that builds the foundation a child needs to transition to independence as soon as he or she is ready, in part by setting clear goals for both your child and family, *and* by placing a particular emphasis on the need for family collaboration and teamwork. To succeed at this approach, you must be willing to commit significant amounts of time, energy, and, yes, kindness, to improving your child's learning experience.

This is no small feat; helping your struggling child can test you at many levels. You may be frustrated by having to relearn things you were taught long ago. You might begin to feel as if you are reliving your own negative experiences from when you were in school. I will provide strategies for how to maintain an awareness of this dynamic so that it does not erode your ability to work productively with your child.

It is a demanding process, but you will come to understand that such deep investments in positive collaboration pay off when your child's capacities do indeed develop. Though it may be time intensive to begin with, in the long run, you'll expend far less time and energy. The old adage "don't work harder, work smarter" is what this book is all about. With its practical approach to restoring a positive mindset to both you and your child, this book will help you restructure school support so it becomes the glue that holds you and your child together, rather than the wedge that divides you.

Part I

An Overview of Language-Based Learning Difficulties

CHAPTER 1

What Is a Language-Based Learning Difficulty?

For as long as there have been schools, there have been children who have struggled to learn. In the past, children who failed at school were often considered lazy, uninterested, or unintelligent. This incorrect assumption has had devastating consequences. Fortunately, as parents, you know that just because your child struggles at school doesn't mean he or she isn't inquisitive, persistent, and capable.

In an effort to better understand and address the overlapping learning disabilities observed in children who struggled in school, the term *language-based learning difficulties* was created. In recent years, it has been used to describe challenges with written and spoken language, mathematics, and attention deficit/hyperactivity disorder (ADHD). The term has also been applied to deficits in skills required for organization, planning, memory, and many related capacities collectively known as *executive functioning skills*.

Understanding this collection of disabilities as a range of interacting challenges is a viewpoint corroborated by Larry Silver, MD, author of *The Misunderstood Child* and *Advice to Parents on ADHD*. Silver urges us to understand common learning differences as a continuum of brain disorders that are frequently found together. The following diagram represents the overlap that is found among common LBLDs.

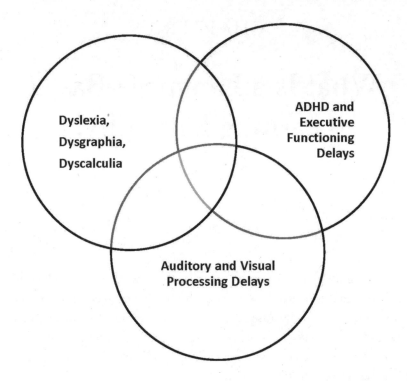

Co-Occurrence of Language-Based Learning Difficulties

Children who struggle to learn commonly have underlying challenges in the areas of language skills development and executive functioning. Challenges in either of these areas—and many children struggle in both—often result in pronounced school difficulties. Indeed, learning disabilities expert Martha Denckla discusses the capacities needed for school success in frank terms: "There are only two chunks of brain function you need to succeed at school. One is your language system, and the other is your executive system" (Denckla 2013).

Examples of the language system	Examples of the executive system
Listening	Attention
Speaking	Focus
Reading	Effort
Writing	Emotional regulation
	Organization
	Planning
	Memory

Unfortunately, for many children with language-based learning difficulties, the development of these two critical systems can be significantly delayed. The demands of school can rapidly overwhelm these children, causing them to quickly fall behind.

A common approach to addressing these disabilities has been to remediate them in isolation, the thinking being that if you reduce a child's struggles to specific skill deficits, you will resolve the more global issues impacting his or her ability to learn. But this reductive approach has not generated the desired results for many children who struggle at school. These children continue to struggle throughout their entire education—and, in many cases, life—despite this highly targeted approach.

Addressing LBLDs in a comprehensive way that also prioritizes the quality of a child's relationship with parents and teachers has been a far more effective approach.

• Sarah's Story

When Sarah and her parents arrived at my office, I was met by a delightful seven-year-old girl with a wide face and a bright smile. Sarah had cheerful brown eyes and curly black hair. As a toddler, Sarah was like most other healthy children her age. She found joy in exploring the world and sharing her discoveries with those around her. At four years old, Sarah had well-developed social skills, she knew how to amuse, and she was deeply inquisitive.

Sarah entered kindergarten at a local public school with a good reputation. From all outward appearances, she was a healthy, normal girl. Sarah played well with her classmates and was well behaved. But her parents began to notice some slight differences relative to her peers. Sarah used fewer words when speaking and had an unusual, if not charming, way of pronouncing her favorite food—"pasghetti"—and her younger brother's name, Michael, which she pronounced "Migle."

Sarah's classmates were able to count up to a hundred, recite the alphabet, spell their names, and tie their shoes. Sarah was unable to do any of these things. She began to notice that she was different, and there was no avoiding the wave of anxiety that swept over her every time she realized that she was falling behind.

Sarah struggled through kindergarten but did well enough that she moved on to first grade. At the start of the year, Sarah was still behind her peers in reading, writing, spelling, and math. Her spoken language skills were delayed. She had difficulty pronouncing a number of common words and some of her friends' names. As the year got under way, it became clear that Sarah frequently did not understand her teacher's directions. She also struggled to follow class lessons and to write letters and numbers clearly and accurately. Sarah's friends quickly learned words to songs, rules to simple board games, and strategies for assembling puzzles, but Sarah struggled to do all of these things.

Sarah's parents tried helping her at home. As they did, they became increasingly aware of their daughter's differences. They brought Sarah to a pediatrician and shared their concerns. The doctor evaluated Sarah's hearing and vision and found they were normal. What could be wrong?

An Overview of Language-Based Learning Difficulties

Sarah's story helps us understand how language-based learning difficulties manifest in the early years of schooling. Not only were Sarah's spoken and written language skills slow to emerge, but she also was having difficulty understanding rudimentary mathematics and accomplishing seemingly age-appropriate tasks, such as tying her shoes and completing puzzles.

Although my general approach is to address LBLDs holistically, it is still helpful to identify the specific challenges children like Sarah often face. In fact, I have organized this book by the commonly used categories that fall under the umbrella term "language-based learning difficulties." When you understand the common challenges experienced by children with LBLDs, you will be able to create a carefully customized and holistic approach to meet your child's unique needs.

What Is Dyslexia?

Dyslexia is primarily a reading disability, but it also impacts many other areas of learning and expression. For this reason, dyslexia is an excellent example of a classification that benefits from a broader understanding under the LBLD umbrella.

Dyslexia has been recognized as a discrete learning disability for many decades. Some dyslexia experts maintain that the term "dyslexia" should be reserved only for people who experience difficulty with reading. Other experts argue that dyslexia describes a broad set of neurological differences that impact a wide range of capacities, including listening, speaking, reading, writing, sequencing, and remembering. All dyslexia experts agree that dyslexia accounts for why some children have more difficulty learning to read than their peers. Even a small delay in reading can, in a few short years, translate into a significant gap between what a child is expected to read at school and what he or she is able to learn from reading.

This gap is often exacerbated for children with dyslexia because they tend to avoid reading. It's an understandable avoidance; for these children, reading is arduous. But avoidance puts them at an even greater disadvantage. This phenomenon is referred to as the "Matthew Effect," a term coined by reading expert Keith Stanovich (1986). In the biblical story of Matthew, the rich get richer and the poor get poorer. In the case of young readers, good readers read more and get better at reading, whereas less-skilled readers read less and fall farther and farther behind their peers. In time, the difference in reading ability can become significant and begin to impact other areas of learning, such as vocabulary development and comprehension. Other capacities, like speaking and writing, can also be influenced by the amount of reading a child does. For many children with dyslexia, delayed progress in these areas diminishes their self-esteem and motivation to complete schoolwork, both of which can further hinder the ability to learn at school.

What Is Dysgraphia?

Children with *dysgraphia* struggle with most aspects of writing. Writing develops along a similar trajectory to reading, where a child moves from basic skills, like recognizing letters, to sophisticated skills, like comprehending. At an early age, a child begins to understand how to form individual letters, spell simple words, and string together words to express thoughts. A breakdown in any of these areas can translate into a writing disability, or dysgraphia.

Additionally, skilled writing requires well-developed executive functioning skills, which is why children with ADHD and executive functioning deficits often struggle to write well. Writing tasks require so many discrete skills that a child who struggles in *any* area of learning or emotional well-being can easily be challenged when attempting to write.

What Is Dyscalculia?

Dyscalculia is a math learning disability that has many similarities to dyslexia and dysgraphia. Children with dyscalculia have difficulty with math at a fundamental level, such as counting, recognizing numbers, forming numbers, understanding money, and telling time. Older children who are unable to perform basic mathematics such as adding, subtracting, multiplying, and dividing can also have dyscalculia.

Like written language, math is governed by many rules that must be followed to be successful. Children with dyscalculia often have difficulty learning and remembering these rules; they therefore require considerably more direct instruction to achieve competency in math. Dyscalculia and dyslexia frequently occur together, which means that children with dyscalculia are also likely to have a hard time understanding written directions, examples, and word problems.

In my practice, I have seen many children identified as having dyscalculia also develop anxiety about math, which further diminishes their ability to learn and perform math-related tasks. This emotional component also needs to be taken into account when determining the type and amount of support you provide your child.

What Are Spoken Language and Visual Processing Challenges?

Generally speaking, being able to process information that is heard or seen is required to learn. I am not describing hearing acuity or seeing acuity, but rather *how information that is seen or heard is processed, retained, and recalled.* Children with LBLDs frequently exhibit significant delays in both spoken language processing and visual processing. As a consequence, they are unable to learn efficiently in a classroom and beyond. Fortunately, there is a lot you can do to help your child if he or she has slowly emerging spoken language and visual processing skills. A key to supporting students with delays in these areas is to provide them with strategies that help them process and remember important things they are being taught.

What Are ADHD and Executive Functioning Disorders?

During the past decade, it has become common to refer to attention deficit/hyperactivity disorder (ADHD) as a deficit in executive functioning skills. Children with ADHD and executive functioning disorders struggle to maintain focus, organize school materials, and manage their time. It's not surprising then that these children struggle to fulfill their academic responsibilities. For example, when ADHD impacts a child's ability to stay focused while reading, the outcome is the same as if he or she were a slowly emerging reader: the child is unable to learn material by reading.

The Ongoing Need for Support

I'd like to confirm what you might already know: that most language-based learning difficulties do not go away. Children with LBLDs continue to need support throughout their entire education. The type and amount of support your child will need will change as his or her capacities develop. Sometimes he or she may only need a little help, but, at other times, your child may need a lot. On occasion, you may find that the support your child needs exceeds what you are capable of providing. In these situations, I encourage you to identify other individuals to partner with in order to provide the additional support your child needs. Sharing the perspectives and strategies offered in this book with those individuals can keep you all on the same page.

Your Child's Learning Environment

Just as it's important to consider your relationship with your child, it is also critical to consider your child's relationship to his or her learning environment. While outside of school it is relatively easy to make the adjustments your child needs, it is not always easy to change school for your child. But all is not hopeless.

It is helpful to consider the work of Deborah Waber and Jane Holmes Bernstein, who suggest we understand academic challenges as a mismatch between the demands and expectations of the school environment and the child's capacities. When there is a mismatch, a catastrophic series of events can quickly follow—and the child is unable to learn. Unfortunately, it is the child who is often viewed as the dysfunctional component, which can result in the child seeing him- or herself as inherently flawed. This results in deeply negative internal thoughts that children can carry for years and sometimes throughout their lives.

Fortunately, a positive collaboration will address mismatches between your child's abilities and his or her environment, and both you and your child will feel bonded and motivated. Importantly, this approach puts you and your child on the same side. In the pages ahead, I will teach you a number of ways you can turn even the most challenging learning environment into a constructive experience for your child.

Conclusion

The umbrella term "language-based learning difficulties" promotes a holistic approach to teaching and supporting children with learning delays, because it takes into account the many overlapping learning challenges they exhibit. This is why this book covers all LBLDs, and it's why I encourage you to read *every chapter*. Even if you believe your child may have dyslexia but not dyscalculia, for example, you may be surprised to find many similarities between both of these learning challenges, along with different applications for the strategies I offer. I want you to think of each chapter as a tool kit that you can pull from to help your child succeed. The strategies I share can be used at any point in your child's schooling.

I'd also like you to start considering the challenges your child may have as a function of his or her environment. When we, as adults, make a conscious effort to better match the environment to the learning and behavioral needs of a struggling child, we have a better chance of helping that child achieve school success.

CHAPTER 2

Correctly Assessing Your Child

In the first part of this chapter, you'll learn the means by which learning and behavioral differences are identified and addressed in public schools. In the second part of this chapter, you'll find out about resources you can draw on to have your child independently assessed if he or she does not attend public school or if you are seeking a second opinion. You'll also discover supplementary resources available to your child regardless of whether he or she attends a public, private, or home school.

Public schools are *required by law* to identify and address learning and behavioral issues that interfere with a child's ability to learn (IDEA 2004). Private, religious, independent, and home schools are not held to the same standard. However, in recent years, some private and religious schools have increased the support and accommodations they are willing to offer their students. Some of these schools are, in fact, specifically designed to address the needs of children with language-based learning difficulties. Other schools are reluctant to acknowledge learning differences among their students or provide any level of support.

Regardless of the type of school your child attends, providing effective help for a child with LBLDs requires a high level of involvement on your part. Your child will benefit greatly by having you as his or her number one advocate. A good place to start is with an understanding of what your son or daughter's challenges are. You probably already have a sense of these difficulties, but when learning challenges become significant and the demands of school consistently exceed your child's capacities, expert advice is often essential.

Here are common indications that your child might benefit from an assessment and intervention:

- Your child dislikes school and frequently asks to stay home.

- Your child appears extremely anxious before school.

- Your child complains about school and hates doing schoolwork.

- Your child appears to be unclear about what he or she is learning at school and hates discussing school.

- Your child routinely gets very low grades.

- Your child struggles to maintain any level of organization.

- You and your child spend many hours completing homework and studying for tests, but he or she is not able to master skills or learn content.

- Your child's teacher reports that your child is struggling to keep up in class.

- Your child's teacher and you have implemented a number of strategies to help resolve your child's struggles, but after a month or two, these strategies are not helping.

If you suspect that your child's skill level is significantly below what it should be, it's time to ask for help. Remember Sarah from the previous chapter? Let's look at how she was impacted by her language-based learning difficulties and what steps were taken to help her.

Sarah's Story (continued)

As first grade got under way, Sarah's parents were surprised by the amount of help their daughter needed to complete even simple homework assignments. The work seemed hard for Sarah and took much longer than they expected. On many occasions, the frustration was more than Sarah could bear, and she frequently shed tears. Her parents' concern was tempered by their observation that Sarah was a smart and well-adjusted girl. She got along with everyone and loved learning about sea creatures.

Sarah's first-grade teacher shared with her parents that she felt Sarah was struggling more than her classmates. After being assured by Sarah's pediatrician that she was normal and healthy, Sarah's parents concluded that their daughter was on a slightly different developmental trajectory and that everything would work out fine. After all, Sarah's mom had been a late bloomer too, and everything worked out well for her.

Halfway through first grade, Sarah's parents were informed that their daughter would begin to receive additional education support through the Response to Intervention (RTI) provision offered by her school. Sarah's parents were encouraged by this news and delighted that their daughter was getting additional support at school.

Levels of Support in Public Schools

Throughout the United States, public schools are required to identify and support children who are struggling to learn. Federal law mandates that all children are entitled to a free and appropriate public education in the least restrictive environment (IDEA 2004). The "least restrictive environment" refers to an environment that is as close to a general education setting as possible. Only when it is determined that a child's educational needs require removal from the general education setting is a child allowed to be placed in a more restrictive environment, such as a resource room, special day class, or special education school.

Response to Intervention (RTI)

Typically, in public schools, when a child begins to struggle, a procedure called *Response to Intervention* (RTI) is followed. RTI has three levels: Tier 1, Tier 2, and Tier 3. Each level offers an increasing amount of support.

RTI Tiers

RTI is a relatively new development in our educational system. It was initiated to avoid the "wait to fail" approach that was previously in place. RTI is a proactive approach that provides support to students before they fall behind.

In the public school system, children who are struggling with class material are provided with additional, targeted support in class. This Tier 1 support typically lasts five to eight weeks, at which point a student is assessed and either returned to regular instruction or moved into Tier 2.

Tier 2 support is small-group, in-class instruction that typically provides remedial and supplementary instruction for fewer than twenty weeks. In elementary school, most of the children who receive Tier 2 support have slowly emerging reading and writing skills (IDEA 2004). Therefore, Tier 2 instruction usually focuses on remedial reading, writing, and spelling instruction. Tier 2 instruction is typically thirty minutes, three to five days per week. Unfortunately, this may not be enough time to adequately address the learning needs of a child with a language-based learning difficulty.

Children who continue to struggle after receiving Tier 2 support are moved into Tier 3. Tier 3 support offers more time, forty-five to 120 minutes each school day, and smaller teacher-to-student ratios, 1:1–3. Tier 3 support typically focuses on remediation and offers more opportunities for work to be done in a scaffolded fashion with the teacher (IDEA 2004).

Both Tier 2 and Tier 3 support are offered without any eligibility requirements aside from teacher observations. For some children, these extra layers of instruction are all that is needed. For many children, particularly those with LBLDs, support beyond RTI is needed.

Sarah's Story (continued)

Although Sarah received Tier 2 support, at the end of the school year, Sarah's teacher recommended that she repeat first grade. After considerable thought, her parents urged her teacher and the school administrators not to hold her back. They knew Sarah would want to be with her friends and pointed out that, physically and mentally, Sarah was a normal, energetic child who got along well with her peers. Reluctantly, the school agreed to promote Sarah.

A Quick Note about Grade Retention

For many years, it was common practice for underachieving children to repeat a grade. This practice is referred to as *grade retention*. It has been the topic of considerable debate. Current evidence suggests that, in most cases, grade retention is not the best course of action (Jimerson 2001). Repetition of course material alone does not necessarily result in mastery, nor does an extra year of developmental maturity necessarily address slowly emerging skills. It has been my experience that grade retention has been successful in some cases. The decision to have a child repeat a grade should only be made after careful consideration.

Sarah's Story (continued)

Even with Tier 2 and then Tier 3 support, Sarah was struggling in second grade. Her frustration and anxiety frequently boiled over, and Sarah would lapse into periods of disruptive behavior. She was frequently kept in at recess for not following class rules and was routinely admonished for not doing her homework. When called on to read, she froze with fear. Her classwork, test, and quiz scores were all far below those of her classmates. She was, however, learning one thing very well: she was not a good student.

Within the first couple of months of second grade, Sarah's parents noticed her downward spiral. They were perplexed. At home, Sarah was the same bright and attentive little girl she had always been. She was kind to her little brother and gracious at family gatherings, where she quickly developed a reputation for being a great entertainer. Sarah was much liked by her friends and had a remarkable capacity to draw fantastical creatures at every opportunity. Why was she such a success as a child but struggling so tremendously as a student? Her parents became deeply concerned about their daughter and what the future may hold for her.

504 Plan

In some instances, when a child struggles to learn at school, a teacher, parent, or school administrator can request the implementation of a 504 Plan. A 504 Plan is based on Section 504 of the Rehabilitation Act of 1973. It can be implemented when a child exhibits learning or behavioral differences that impede his or her ability to learn. Eligibility for a 504 Plan does not require a specific diagnosis. It does require a school meeting, but it only involves parents, teachers, and a school administrator. A 504 Plan is a written set of accommodations that offer a child small adjustments to classroom instruction (Rehabilitation Act of 1973). These adjustments can include preferential seating to be closer to the teacher, extended time on tests, test locations with reduced distractions, reduced homework, support with note taking, and assistance fulfilling other in-class responsibilities.

A 504 Plan is implemented as long as the child's educational needs can be met in a general educational setting. If a child needs support beyond what the 504 Plan provides, the child will be considered for an IEP. A 504 Plan does not identify a specific learning or behavioral disability; therefore, simply having a 504 Plan does not make a student eligible for special education services, such as learning specialist support, resource room help, placement in a special day class, or an alternative learning environment. 504 Plans do not require that a child be evaluated to determine if he or she is eligible for special education services; this makes them fairly quick and easy to implement.

Sarah's Story (continued)

Sarah's parents' concern grew following the first parent-teacher conference of the school year. Her second-grade teacher, Ms. Price, shared with Sarah's parents that their daughter was struggling to keep up in class. She explained that Sarah always appeared lost and was unable to follow class instructions. Ms. Price said Sarah rarely raised her hand to answer questions, and, when called on, she had a very difficult time organizing her thoughts. The teacher said Sarah needed many reminders not to draw during class time or look out the window when she should be doing her seatwork. Sarah's desk was a mess, and she was constantly losing her possessions. To their surprise, Sarah's parents learned that homework assignments they had done with their daughter were never submitted.

Sarah's parents had had enough. With the help of Ms. Price, they requested that the school district evaluate Sarah to try to understand why she was struggling. Within several weeks, a school district psychologist had completed a comprehensive educational evaluation of Sarah and provided her parents with a report detailing her learning characteristics.

The testing showed that Sarah's reading, writing, spelling, and math skills were significantly below what would be expected considering her age. This indicated that Sarah met the criteria for a specific learning disability (SLD), *which includes learning issues such as dyslexia. The testing also revealed that Sarah had pronounced deficits in some areas of attention and memory. This indicated that Sarah also met the criteria for* other health impaired (OHI), *which includes issues such as ADHD. These designations, SLD and OHI, are two of the thirteen eligibility criteria covered by the Individuals with Disabilities Education Act (IDEA) of 2004. By meeting these eligibility criteria, Sarah was now able to receive an IEP and access to special education services.*

Individualized Education Plan (IEP)

When a child exhibits pronounced learning and behavioral differences at school, a 504 Plan may be insufficient. In this case, a child's parents or the school can seek an *individualized education plan*. Access to IEP is mandated under IDEA. Among other things, IDEA guarantees that every child receives a free and appropriate public education (IDEA 2004).

During an assessment for IEP eligibility, a child will be assigned an evaluator by the school. This individual is a school psychologist who is trained to administer a variety of educational and psychological assessments. In some cases, the school will request additional testing to better understand the learning or behavioral challenges a child exhibits. This testing is conducted by qualified specialists and is referred to as an Independent Educational Evaluation (IEE).

The process by which a child receives an IEP and qualifies for special education support is complex and involves many school personnel. Here are the steps leading to an IEP:

1. The child is identified as struggling at school and unable to access curriculum.

2. The child is referred for an evaluation.

3. The evaluation determines that the child has a significant disability that adversely affects his or her ability to access curriculum.

4. The disability meets one of the thirteen IDEA eligibility categories (see chart).

5. An IEP meeting is convened to determine what additional support the child needs in order to access curriculum. This meeting includes the following individuals:

   School psychologist

   General education teacher

   Special education teacher

   Leading school administrator

   School nurse

   The child

   The child's parents

   Any additional individuals the parents would like to invite

The IEP stipulates supplementary support services and other instructional accommodations needed by the child. The IEP also includes a list of specific learning goals and a timeline in which the goals should be achieved (IDEA 2004). If the parents feel that the support offered is insufficient, they can request more. If this request is denied, the parents can file an appeal and seek additional support through the appeals process. *An IEP does not provide a specific diagnosis of your child's learning challenges. The goal of an IEP is to determine your child's eligibility to receive special education.*

The Thirteen Eligibility Categories Covered by the Individuals with Disabilities Education Act

1. **Specific learning disability (SLD)** means a disorder in one or more of the basic psychological processes involved in understanding or in using language—spoken or written—that may adversely affect a child's ability to listen, think, speak, read, write, spell, or do math. SLDs include dyslexia, dysgraphia, and dyscalculia.

2. **Other health impairment (OHI)** includes a wide range of physical illnesses and health issues, including limited mental alertness and heightened mental alertness, that interfere with memory and attention. ADHD is considered an OHI.

3. **Autism** means a developmental disability significantly affecting verbal and nonverbal communication and social interaction. Other characteristics include engagement in repetitive activities, resistance to environmental change or change in daily routines, and unusual responses to sensory experiences.

4. **Speech or language impairment** includes stuttering, impaired articulation, a language impairment, or a voice impairment.

5. **Intellectual disability** means significantly lower intellectual abilities and significant challenges with social and life skills.

6. **Emotional disturbance (ED)** covers a broad range of mental disorders such as pervasive depression, anxiety, and fears. It also includes disorders such as schizophrenia. ED includes inappropriate behaviors or feelings, and the inability to build or maintain satisfactory interpersonal relationships with peers.

7. **Visual impairment**, including blindness, means an impairment in vision that, even with correction, adversely affects a child's educational performance.

8. **Deafness** means a hearing impairment that is so severe that the child is impaired in processing information through hearing.

9. **Hearing impairment** means a dysfunction in hearing that adversely affects a child's educational performance but that is not included under the definition of deafness in this section.

10. **Deaf-blindness** means hearing and visual impairments.

11. **Orthopedic impairment** means a severe orthopedic disability that adversely affects a child's educational performance.

12. **Traumatic brain injury** means an acquired injury to the brain caused by an external physical force.

13. **Multiple disabilities** means concomitant impairments (such as intellectual disability–blindness or intellectual disability–orthopedic impairment).

This summary is based on Section 34 CFR § 300.8 in IDEA (2012).

This sheet is also available for download at the website for this book: http://www.newharbinger.com/40989. See the very back of this book for details on how to access it.

Many of the services available to a child through his or her IEP are provided in the context of different settings:

Push-in support is when a special education teacher provides support to one or more students in the context of a regular education classroom. This support can occur for part or all of the class.

A resource room is typically a room on campus where a child goes to receive help on a specific skill or in a specific subject. This support from a resource teacher can range from additional help on a class assignment to remedial skill instruction to all instruction in a specific subject, like reading. Children may spend anywhere from one to seven hours a week in the resource room. Resource room placement should be considered when a child who has qualified under an IEP needs explicit remedial instruction in reading, writing, spelling, and/or math, or when the content of a regular class exceeds his or her processing capacities.

A special day class is almost always designated for children with significant learning delays and behavioral differences. Children in special day class spend the entire school day in this class, receiving instruction in all subjects. Placement in a special day class should be considered when the general education program does not meet a child's social, emotional, and/or learning needs.

Special education day and residential schools vary enormously depending on the population of students they serve. Some schools are designed for children with severe learning and behavioral differences, while other schools are designed to serve only students with LBLDs. The range is so wide that school placement is best determined through research and the advice of a special education school placement specialist.

What If I Disagree with the Evaluation or Plan Offered?

If you disagree with the findings of the school's evaluation or the supplementary support the school offers, there is an appeals process you can follow. You can also seek an independent evaluation to help you better determine what may underlie your child's learning and behavioral differences.

Private Assessments

There are few resources more valuable to a student and his or her parents than a well-conducted, independent assessment and written report. I have had the good fortune of working with some of the very best clinicians who conduct testing and write reports and recommendations to address the social, emotional, and learning needs of children who are struggling in school. Understanding your child's learning disabilities will help you and your child's teachers develop a support plan that works. For many parents, working with a clinician who is trained to diagnose learning disabilities is the most efficient route toward identifying their child's learning profile and needs.

Many parents seek an independent evaluation by a private provider, such as a reading specialist, a speech and language specialist, an educational psychologist, or a neuropsychologist. School districts may or may not recognize the findings of an independent assessment. Even if the independent evaluation is not used to garner school support, it may provide additional information for parents seeking support beyond the services offered by their child's school or for parents seeking a second opinion as to the underlying causes of their child's struggles.

For children enrolled in private schools, an independent evaluation may be required to gain accommodations and adjustments in the classroom. Prior to seeking an independent evaluation, parents should be aware that there are many different types of evaluations and many different individuals who provide them.

A private assessment for your child is recommended if he or she is struggling at school and you want to get a better understanding of why. (In many cases, a school assessment will provide sufficient information to appropriately address your child's social, emotional, and learning needs. School assessments are intended to determine if a child qualifies for special education support or therapeutic treatment within the context of school; they are not intended to diagnose specific learning or behavioral disabilities.) In order to determine if a child has a specific learning or behavioral disability, a private assessment is generally required.

Neuropsychological and Psychoeducational Assessments

Prior to arranging comprehensive testing, a good first step is seeking the input of an individual who has expertise in the area that concerns you. For example, if your child is struggling with reading and writing, first get an informal evaluation from a reading and writing specialist. If this individual identifies a significant issue, then you may consider seeking a more detailed evaluation from a psychologist or neuropsychologist.

The most widely accepted form of learning and behavioral assessments is a neuropsychological evaluation conducted by a neuropsychologist. A neuropsychologist is a professional who holds a doctorate-level degree in psychology and has received specific training in the area of neuropsychological testing. In addition to neuropsychologists, there are a number of other clinicians, such as educational psychologists and clinical psychologists, who can provide excellent information concerning your child's learning and behavioral needs.

When seeking an educational, psychological, psychoeducational, or neuropsychological evaluation for your child, bear in mind there are many different professionals with widely varying qualifications who offer these services. Many trained educators can administer a basic screening assessment to determine a child's skill in reading, writing, or math. Keep in mind that many other assessments require expertise. Carefully vet any clinician you are considering. There are a number of trusted sources who can help you identify a qualified professional to assess your child:

- School administrator

- School psychologist

- School counselor

- Pediatrician

- Psychologist/psychiatrist

- Therapist or clinician (MFT/LCSW)

- Websites for professional organizations, such as the American Psychological Association and the American Speech-Language-Hearing Association

Once you have identified an individual who you might like to conduct the assessment, devote some time to research his or her qualifications. In vetting clinicians, you want to know:

- Where they earned their qualifications

- What their specialties are

- How long they have been in practice

- What the fee is for testing

- When they can see your child

- How quickly they will provide results after testing

- If they will provide a report in a format you can use to seek accommodations

- If they are affiliated with any professional organizations

Most testing is carried out over several days. Each day might involve several hours of testing and assessment. Evaluations generally begin with an interview with the parents about their child. The evaluator gathers as much historical information as he or she can about the child. The evaluator then gathers information about the child by administering tests, having parents and teachers complete questionnaires, and observing the child's behavior throughout the testing process.

Most comprehensive evaluations assess the following areas:

- General intellect

- Reading and writing skills

- Math skills

- Attention

- Learning and memory

- Visual processing

- Auditory processing

- Social skills

Once testing is completed, the evaluator will create a profile of the child's learning and behavioral characteristics. This information is used to generate a written report about the child. This report provides insights into why the child exhibits the learning and behavioral characteristics that are of concern to the parents. The report also provides parents with a number of recommendations to help support the child at school, at home, and out in the world.

The evaluator might also recommend that the child receive support from specialists in different areas of learning and behavior. Here are some of the specialists who might be recommended:

Speech therapists address a broad range of speaking and listening skills, including the physical aspects of speech: pronunciation, stuttering, tone, pace, and cadence. They also work with children on social pragmatics: initiating conversation, changing topics in conversation, maintaining conversation, and understanding figurative language. When children struggle to understand what is said or communicate what they want to say, a speech therapist should be considered.

Occupational therapists help children develop a range of fine and gross motor skills. As occupational therapy relates to schoolwork, support for fine motor skill development may be needed for handwriting, drawing, and using scissors. Outside of school, fine motor development is necessary for basic life skills, such as brushing teeth, tying shoes, buttoning clothing, and using utensils. Gross motor skills involve muscle tone and coordination. Children who need help with gross motor skills benefit from direct instruction in tasks such as folding laundry; making beds; gathering books; cleaning backpacks; and developing muscle strength, hand-eye coordination, and balance.

Reading specialists help children who have slowly emerging reading skills. There is strong evidence that early identification and intervention for children who exhibit delayed reading skills will be helpful, but it does not mean that the child's reading challenges are over. Frequently, when the demands of reading become more complex in high school, children who had reading challenges at a young age are likely to exhibit reading challenges again (Denckla 2013). Also, it is important to remember that although many types of reading instruction can improve *automaticity*—the ability to recognize words in print instantly—comprehension requires different skills and should be addressed separately.

Math specialists are helpful when a child is chronically struggling or a parent feels that his or her child's school is not providing sufficient instruction. Struggles with math usually involve one or more of three main categories: The first category is the capacity to accurately understand number sense and number representation—how numbers are written and what they signify. The second category is related to language comprehension—struggling to convert math word problems into numeric equations; struggles in this category offer an excellent example of how a learning disability in one area, such as dyslexia, can impact learning in another area, math. The third main category is difficulty grasping the underlying concepts of common procedures, such as the concept of borrowing from the tens or hundreds column when performing subtraction. Often, manipulatives, modeling, and specialized instruction are needed to adequately convey concepts. Math specialists can identify why a child is struggling with math and then develop and implement a math enrichment program.

ADHD coaches address the organizational and time management challenges that children with ADHD face. ADHD coaches can work with children and their parents to develop and implement strategies that address a child's underlying challenges. Parent participation is essential because many of the strategies involve high levels of ongoing support from a parent or a tutor.

Educational therapists provide remedial instruction, promote study skills, conduct educational assessments, evaluate educational needs, determine appropriate types of support and intervention, and function as an advocate and case manager for students with a wide range of learning differences (Ficksman and Adelizzi 2010). Currently, educational therapy is not a licensed profession. That said, some educational therapists carry certifications issued by organizations that offer training and require the adherence to professional standards and ethical codes.

Academic tutors can also be a very useful resource. Tutoring as a profession is growing rapidly, and there are many tutors who are excellent at supporting not only students but also parents. Working together, you and the tutor may be just the arrangement of support that is needed to help your child navigate the demands of school, learn successfully, and get good grades. Be sure the academic tutor is sufficiently experienced and qualified to work with your child.

Conclusion

When a child begins to exhibit signs that he or she is not progressing according to standardized timelines, it is natural for parents to be concerned and offer help in every way they can. As a parent, you are in the best position to advocate for your child at school. When your child is not able to manage the demands of school, you can help by establishing and maintaining regular communication with your child's teacher. By working collaboratively with your child's teacher, you can seek additional levels of support in the classroom.

If you need to move beyond the classroom to seek support for your child, you have a variety of options available to you. If your child attends public school, you can draw on the resources provided by a 504 Plan or an IEP. You can also seek the input, advice, and support of independent evaluators and learning specialists to understand and address your child's needs. Keep in mind that children rarely develop skills across several areas at the same time. In following a specialist's recommendations, it will be important to prioritize the most significant issue. For example, if your child with ADHD is failing his or her math class, it will probably be more beneficial to work with a math specialist than an ADHD coach until progress in math has been made.

In the next chapter, I offer my rationale for why it is beneficial to address learning and behavioral challenges in a holistic way. As you will see, a key facet of this approach is to engage in highly collaborative support in the context of a healthy, positive relationship with your child.

CHAPTER 3

A Kinder Way to Support Your Child

The kind of help I advocate for children with language-based learning difficulties requires a profound lifestyle shift for the whole family—*not* a set of quick fixes. Mine is a collaborative method that builds the foundation a child needs to transition to independence as soon as he or she is ready, in part by setting clear goals for the child and family *and* by emphasizing the need for family collaboration and teamwork. To succeed at this approach, parents must be willing to commit significant amounts of time, energy, and, yes, *kindness*, to improving their child's learning experience.

When I begin working with any child, I ask him or her a series of questions. The questions have been virtually the same for many years. My first question is always: "Have you ever heard of a shooting star?" (I was a science teacher and I am fascinated by astronomy.) This leads to a brief conversation about a topic that is interesting to most students. After a level of comfort has been established, I ask, "In all of your years at school, which year was your favorite?" When the child identifies his or her favorite year, I ask what made the year so special. This question elicits exactly the same answer no matter the child's age, gender, or learning needs. Day after day, year after year, children respond that the year was their favorite *because the teacher was "nice."*

When I ask what "nice" means, the children's descriptions make it clear that the teacher displayed a genuine interest in them and seemed to like them. The teacher was warm and patient. The teacher was empathetic and prioritized healthy relationships. In short, the teacher was *kind*.

Mindful awareness practices teach us to be curious and pay attention, to be reflective and appreciative, and to share with others what we observe and feel. This approach to life has always struck me as a formula for kindness, a crucial ingredient in my approach to helping children with LBLDs. Paying attention begins with having a sincere interest in your child's life in and out of school. When you are curious, attuned, and attentive to your child, you are being kind. When you are paying attention during homework, you are able to know when your child needs help, patience, silence, or a break. You are also able to create opportunities for your child to demonstrate what he or she knows and to structure your interactions in ways that will further encourage your child's motivation for learning.

By paying attention, you may also be astonished not only by how hard many homework assignments are but also by how gifted your child is. I believe you will become deeply aware of the monumental effort that your child is actually putting forth. You will be able to appreciate your child even more and share with him or her what you observe and have been astonished by. And if you aren't already, I believe you will be more enthusiastic to have this opportunity to be your child's teammate.

All people want to be treated kindly, and it is almost impossible to be too kind to children. This is not a small point. Every ounce of kindness matters, especially for children who have LBLDs. I should know: during my own years-long struggle with school, I often felt that my teachers were angry at me because I wasn't learning quickly enough. And when I sensed any exasperation from them, I, in turn, grew angry and couldn't learn at all.

But here and there, I had a handful of teachers who treated me with patience and respect. Their kindness helped me learn in a way that anger and intimidation never did. I may not have always done the work these kind teachers wanted me to do, but I did indeed learn from them.

And perhaps the greatest lesson I learned was how to be compassionate when children are struggling. This awareness is critical, because it is now well established that in a state of stress or anxiety, a child's ability to learn is greatly diminished. Unfortunately, many children with

LBLDs are in a chronic state of anxiety. For these reasons, I cannot emphasize enough that reducing stress and anxiety at school and at home when working with your child is essential when trying to achieve learning outcomes. Additional research indicates that a positive state of mind promotes *neuroplasticity*, the sculpting and shaping of the brain required for skill development and learning. Everything you do as a parent to help your child feel safe, secure, calm, and regulated will promote better learning. Anger, intimidation, threats, and demands that exceed capacities undermine development and learning (Forbes and Post 2009).

This knowledge—that compassion and kindness can make a tangible difference in the lives of struggling children—forms the core of my approach to helping children with LBLDs succeed in school. For this approach to be successful, you will need to:

- prioritize the health of your relationship with your child over the demands of school; and

- provide the amount of support your child needs to complete homework and study for tests and quizzes.

When you do these two things, your child will be able to complete homework, learn more, and, ultimately, get better grades.

Making kindness work in real life means shifting your mindset to treat with reverence the relationship you have with your child and the opportunity to help him or her. Patience and attentiveness are fundamental elements of reverence. With repeated practice, brains actually become wired for reverence (Lutz et al. 2004). And once you have internally primed yourself, it's quite easy to make kindness the foundation of all, or at least most, of your interactions with your child. I believe that the more you prioritize having a healthy relationship with your child, the better off your son or daughter will be throughout the rest of his or her life.

This is the lifestyle shift my approach encourages families to make. It is not a remedy with a timetable but rather a type of support that is intended to be ongoing—and it only works when it is embraced by the whole family. Is it quick? No. Is it easy? Definitely not. Does it work? Absolutely.

Your Relationship With Your Child Is More Important Than Schoolwork

When I ask children to share their positive school experiences and memories, I do so to remind them that at one point they were happy while learning, and that learning can be enjoyable. I would like to remind you, as a parent, too. Your child has enjoyed learning and can enjoy learning with you.

We run into problems when we allow schoolwork to undermine the relationships we have with our children. It is easy to see how this happens: parents become short tempered when an assignment is due, anxious when material hasn't been mastered in time for a test, and disheartened when learning takes a long time.

Your child's capacities are developing on a timeline that is unique to him or her. Forcing children to do something they are not ready to do diminishes their self-worth. In fact, the anxiety chronic among so many children who have LBLDs results from their knowledge that the demands placed on them exceed their capacities. When these children face reasonable expectations, they are highly motivated and engaged. They feel acknowledged and connected, and their success breeds further success.

Comparing one student to another and arriving at a conclusion about what is developmentally normal or appropriate based on this comparison does not appear to be productive. It makes a presumption that there is such a thing as "average." Harvard scientist Todd Rose has challenged the practice of making these statistical comparisons, and he recommends that we appreciate every student. Because there is considerable variation in the rate at which all students develop, these variations do not imply inherent deficit but rather a reflection of a poor fit between the student and his or her environmental demands (Rose 2016).

It's also important to remember that children are consistently inconsistent. Just because they are able to do something one day does not mean they will be able to do it again the next day. By understanding this from the outset, you can be more at ease when helping your child and less frustrated when you need to provide support for something you thought your child could do on his or her own. Let me tell you: if it were easy for your child to do something on his or her own, it would be done!

It is essential to realize that supporting children with language-based learning difficulties often means helping with schoolwork *daily* from elementary school through high school and even into the early years of college. This is why it is so important to prioritize your relationship over schoolwork. You will be working together a lot, over a long period of time. The stronger and healthier your relationship is with your child, the more likely it is you will be a successful team.

Collaboration Is Not "Enabling"

In my practice, I frequently encounter two types of children: children who feel ashamed of themselves because they get bad grades, and children who feel ashamed of themselves because they need a lot of assistance from their parents to complete their homework. Neither needs to be true. Receiving assistance is the basis of a strong, healthy, collaborative relationship between a parent and a child.

All human relationships are based on dependence, which can be healthy or unhealthy. We make dependence healthy by recognizing it for what it is: receiving *necessary* support. If you want to help your child become independent, provide him or her with the help he or she needs. Withholding support when he or she needs it is a sure way to make your child dependent for the rest of his or her life.

Parents are innately attached to their children. It is easy to sublimate this connection when helping with homework because we have been taught that helping with homework is cheating or that if you help your child he or she will always be dependent on you. The biggest concern I hear parents raise is: "My child needs to be able to do _____ on his or her own." Let me assure you that your child will naturally seek independence when he or she is ready if you have provided the scaffolding and modeling needed for him or her to develop skills and the confidence to try.

When you work closely on schoolwork with your child, and when you provide that support in a positive way, you are being kind. When you help your child feel comfortable with getting support, you will be able to see that his or her struggles are legitimate. You will also be in a position to reassure your child by recognizing his or her gifts and contributions, and letting him or her know those qualities are great resources now and always. Most important, by adopting the kinder approach I outline in this book, you will be able to communicate your optimism for your child's future. No one has ever been disappointed by the optimism he or she has been shown by another. You cannot underestimate the value of optimism, especially for a child who has been struggling in school.

Working collaboratively will benefit both you and your child. He or she will find that school-related tasks can be done more quickly and with better learning outcomes. Working with your child will allow you to assess his or her skill level so you can adjust your support as needed. Providing support that meets your son or daughter's needs will boost his or her motivation to work hard and learn. Because it feels good to be successful!

Acclaimed education experts Robert Brooks, Sam Goldstein, and Richard Lavoie have observed that a child's level of motivation is a more critical factor in determining how and what he or she learns than almost all other considerations (Brooks and Goldstein 2001, Lavoie 2007). As we move our instructional approach to one that focuses on collaboration, we are able to foster the positive interpersonal relationships that improve a child's motivation to learn. When help is provided in this way, it is *not* enabling.

Slowly, as you see your child is ready, you will need to scaffold less and less. Facilitating homework for a child who has language-based learning difficulties will *not* prevent the child from acquiring skills—in fact, I have always been struck by how naturally a child will integrate new skills once he or she has mastered them. But until then, support is required.

The Role of Bypass Strategies

In the early grades, some children with LBLDs are not identified as struggling learners because they have not fallen significantly behind their peers in reading, writing, math, and executive functioning skills. This is why many children with dyslexia, dysgraphia, dyscalculia, or ADHD are not identified until upper elementary school, at which point they may be quite far behind their peers in basic skill development.

The graph below illustrates the widening gap between *expected* skill development and *delayed* skill development experienced by children with LBLDs. This graph can apply to skill development in any area, including reading, writing, math, or executive functioning. In particular, you can see that by upper middle school and early high school, children with LBLDs can be many years behind their peers.

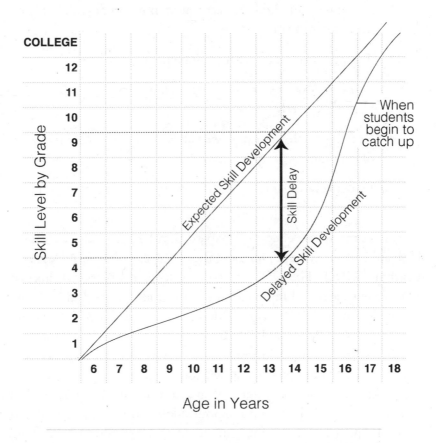

Skill Development Discrepancy

Unfortunately, specific skill remediation, especially for older children, takes a long time. It is nearly impossible for an older child with a pronounced disability to catch up to his or her peers quickly. Despite the wide skill gap, students with LBLDs are still capable of learning high-level content, and we must balance the need these students have for remedial instruction with the equally important need to access and learn high-level content. To do this, we have to bypass slowly emerging skills. Throughout this book, I offer many bypass strategies, including:

- Reading textbooks aloud and checking for understanding

- Engaging your child in a conversation to develop and organize ideas before writing

- Taking dictation for writing assignments

- Using graph paper and drawing columns to keep math solutions aligned correctly

- Reading math word problems aloud and converting them into illustrations

- Proactively organizing homework time to promote efficiency and completion

In recent years, education expert David Rose and his team at Harvard University have promoted the concept of Universal Design for Learning (UDL). The UDL approach includes instructional practices that present ideas and information to each student based on his or her unique learning characteristics (Meyer, Rose, and Gordon 2014). You can utilize principles of UDL by experimenting with instructional approaches that your child responds to and by actively engaging your child in the learning process. When you draw on your innate creative capacities, I am confident you'll be able to find effective ways to help your child learn and develop important skills. In chapter 9, I offer an array of approaches to helping your child process and understand things he or she is being taught.

It's important to remember that even as your child's skills improve, your assistance will still be needed—even through high school. LBLDs are persistent. Furthermore, your child will face other challenges that will exceed his or her capacities, such as busy schedules, more demanding coursework, and larger amounts of homework. To support you in the ongoing years, additional bypass strategies in handy checklist form can be found on this book's website: http://www.newharbinger.com/40989.

Subskill Coupling: The Underlying Problem

Many years ago, while teaching children with language-based learning difficulties, I noticed that if an assignment contained a task that exceeded a student's skill level, a disastrous sequence of events soon followed. One slowly emerging skill, like reading, led to the inability to read directions, which led to the inability to complete an assignment, which led to a failing grade. One problem led to another, and the child quickly spun out of control.

In the early 1990s, I gave this phenomenon the name "subskill coupling." Simply put, subskill coupling occurs when one slowly emerging capacity greatly exacerbates another slowly emerging capacity to the point that an assignment cannot be completed. It is one of the most significant, unrecognized obstacles to a child's ability to complete homework and learn. For example, in upper elementary school, there is frequently an expectation that children are already capable readers. If the student is not a skilled reader, however, assignments that require reading become virtually impossible. So when a skill is lagging, we need to support it by using bypass strategies.

In addition to reading, there are a vast number of other skills children need to complete homework, including writing, planning, time management, organization, and attention. If a child hasn't mastered all of these skills, as many children with LBLDs have not, it is unrealistic to expect them to manage homework independently.

I encounter subskill coupling in my work frequently. For example, a few years ago I began working with a student who had been failing her weekly vocabulary tests. I discovered that every Monday the teacher put a list of ten vocabulary words on the board. Students were required to write the words down, look up their meanings, and be prepared to spell and define the words correctly on a test at the end of the week. My student had both dyslexia and ADHD. Unfortunately, the many subskills involved such as copying words, looking words up, learning to spell words, and memorizing their meanings overwhelmed her.

The primary learning objective of this exercise was for the students to increase their vocabulary. But my student had great difficulty copying the words from the board accurately. This in turn prevented her from finding the definitions and learning how to spell the words correctly. To scaffold the learning objective, I proactively obtained a list of the weekly vocabulary words, provided my student with their meanings, and supported her with the steps required to learn how to spell and define them. With the high level of support I provided her, she successfully learned the meanings of these words, which was the primary objective, and performed well on her tests.

As your child's skills are developing, it is crucial that you help him or her approach homework assignments systematically, step by step, and that you give yourself permission to help with the tasks that exceed his or her capacities. Asking a child who has not yet mastered all of the skills schoolwork requires without support is like expecting someone to learn how to square dance at the same time he is learning to play the fiddle. It's too much to do all at once.

Steps for Preventing Subskill Coupling

1.   *Identify the primary learning objective of each assignment.* Is the assignment designed to boost your child's vocabulary or improve his or her spelling skills? When you understand the primary learning objective, you will have an easier time helping your child achieve success on his or her terms. For example, if your child has a weekly vocabulary quiz, find out what the words are, write them out clearly yourself, and provide your child with a concise definition for each. (Remember: learning the vocabulary words is the primary learning objective here; your job is to remove any additional barriers to learning those words.) During the week, review the vocabulary with your child, making the task of memorization as fun as possible: set the definitions to music, draw pictures, use flashcards—whatever method your child enjoys most. By bypassing slowly emerging skills, you can help your child learn the vocabulary, which is the primary objective.

2. *Compartmentalize each assignment into step-by-step tasks.* Help your child focus on the aspects of the assignment that will help him or her achieve the primary learning objective. This alone may be enough to make the assignment feasible. It may also be that specific tasks exceed your child's capacities or draw attention away from the primary learning objective. In that case, take an active role in supporting those tasks. For example, if your child has a history assignment that involves writing, a presentation, and a construction project, you should carefully study the assignment and consider how it can be broken down into achievable steps. At times you will have to function as the organizer, the planner, and the time manager. For many children with LBLDs, these critical capacities have not yet emerged.

3. *Use bypass strategies to achieve the primary learning objective.* If it's clear that a reading component exceeds your child's capacities, read to your child. If writing is difficult for your child, allow him or her to dictate to you. Do your best to help your child achieve the primary learning objective or assignment requirement. Work on developing the other skills at a different time. For example, if your child needs to complete an algebra problem that requires multiplication, and your child's multiplication skills are emerging slowly, then do the multiplication for your child or allow him or her to use a calculator. This allows your child to focus his or her energy on using formulas and the order of operations (the primary learning objective) correctly.

Note: This document is also available for download at the website for this book: http://www.newharbinger.com/40989

If you involve yourself in addressing subskill coupling, you will allow your child to manage the demands of homework when they exceed what he or she is capable of. You will also help your child learn specific study skills and achieve the teacher's primary learning objective. Parents often doubt their ability to provide homework support, but I believe if the approach is right, no one could be better for the job than a parent. Recognizing when subskill coupling is occurring and doing something about it will allow your child to excel in all areas of learning and school. Furthermore, it will foster the kind of positive collaboration that promotes learning and skill development.

Conclusion

I wish it were possible to say that if you work with your child collaboratively for six weeks or six months, he or she will acquire all of the capacities needed to manage the demands of school independently. But the truth is that many children with LBLDs need years of collaborative support to contend with school while their written language and executive functioning skills are emerging.

Providing your child with the help that he or she needs doesn't mean you are hindering skill development. In fact, there are few things that hinder skill development more than withholding support when it is needed. Forcing children to contend with overwhelming situations on their own diminishes learning, reduces confidence, increases anxiety, and raises the level of conflict in the home. When you confidently and proactively support your child in all the areas where help is needed, you will provide him or her with the fastest route to learning, skill development, and independence.

By using bypass strategies to resolve the challenges of subskill coupling, your child's efforts will be spent on what they should be spent on: learning content, acquiring study skills, completing homework, and being prepared for tests and quizzes. Collaborating with your child on homework will also show your child that you are a consistent, reliable source of support. The level of kindness that characterizes your relationship with your child should not be forsaken while doing homework but rather called upon and leveraged as a means of managing the demands of school and learning important skills. Provide the help your child needs and you will both be deeply rewarded.

Part II

Succeeding at School

CHAPTER 4

Forming a Strong Bond with Your Child

Doing poorly in school traumatizes children. This is a fact that parents who watch their children struggle with schoolwork on a daily basis understand better than anyone. But even parents may not realize just how lasting this trauma can be. We know that children with pronounced language-based learning difficulties exhibit chronically elevated levels of stress (Panicker and Chelliah 2016) and that stress is disruptive to brain development and learning (Sapolsky 2004). There's no doubt that school-related stress is traumatic, but as much as they might want to help, many parents don't know where to begin.

Helping children with LBLDs doesn't require a flashy new reading program or an intensive math curriculum. There is just one requirement: establish (or reestablish) a healthy, positive relationship with your child. Though building this relationship can be challenging, an open, affirmative connection between you and your child is the greatest gift your child can receive. Not only are healthy relationships the most effective route to promoting learning and skill development, but they also provide opportunities to address the psychological trauma children experience when they struggle in school. Because an essential step in ending the struggle with an LBLD is to *help the child heal from the trauma of school-related failure.*

In this chapter, I'll share my experiences working with a boy whose language-based learning difficulties resulted in acute school-related trauma. I'll explain how you can stay calm and create opportunities for a secure bond with your son or daughter. And I'll show you how it is possible to reshape your child's internal thought process to rebuild his or her self-esteem.

What I will not do, however, is recommend a rigid adherence to any one strategy. Your strategies will, for the most part, result from listening to what your unique child needs and to the parental instincts you are often told to ignore. It has been my experience that when parents listen to these instincts, their relationship with their child improves dramatically. If I've learned one thing in my three decades of working with children, it is this: *positive collaboration is the most effective way to improve academic performance and heal a broken spirit.* In my experience, nothing else even comes close.

Get started by exploring these seven steps to creating a closer and more compassionate bond with your child. Some of them may bring up uncomfortable feelings or seem time consuming. But hang in there. Your efforts will eventually result in a stronger connection and a more confident child.

Step 1: Identify the Problem

At some point, you suspected that there might be a problem with your child. But what is the problem, exactly? Let's hear about a boy who was struggling—and how we pinpointed the source of his struggles.

• *Nate's Story*

Some years ago, I started working with a boy, an only child, who was being raised by his mother. Nate's language-based learning difficulties were pronounced, and he was behind in reading, writing, and math. He was anxious, angry, and volatile.

When we weren't discussing school, Nate was an engaging and curious child. He was quick to offer his help with any chore, showed remarkable sensitivity to other people's feelings, and had incredible powers of observation. But the mention of schoolwork brought about a violent reaction in Nate—a clear indication that he was in tremendous pain. What was going on with Nate?

Maybe you have an idea of what's going on with your child. Maybe educators or clinical professionals have weighed in. Maybe not. Either way, it's time to find out what exactly is going on by taking your first step.

Explore the problem. You can be your own investigator by compassionately asking yourself some important questions:

Are things as good as they could be? Identify the qualities in life you are seeking for yourself and your child. If you are aware of key elements that can be improved upon, it is time to take action.

How does my child feel? Children are often reluctant to express what they are feeling. At other times, they are unaware that their experiences are less than optimal. What do you observe in your child? Which situations trigger difficult behavior? Which situations trigger happiness, curiosity, enthusiasm, and perseverance in your child? Find time to explore with your child how he or she is feeling. Perhaps you have noticed that your child does not speak in a positive way about school. You might want to point out this observation to your child and explore it together.

How do I feel? Are you enjoying your experience as a parent? If not, what aspects of parenting do you find challenging? For many parents, school-related issues underlie much of the dissatisfaction they have with parenting. Try to identify what those issues are and begin to think through ways of bringing about positive change.

What have I tried? If you have been using the same strategy for a long time without any results, it might be time to move in a new direction. For example, if rewards, punishments, and strict schedules aren't working, try something different.

What should I try next? There are plenty of strategies in this book, but it takes time to find the strategies that will work best for your child. Along the way, talk with individuals who can guide you toward a better understanding of your child's challenges.

Who can help? There are many professionals who can offer help and guidance when you feel overwhelmed by your child's LBLD challenges. Your pediatrician will likely have suggestions. You can also ask a trusted person at your child's school. A good starting point is a child psychologist or an educational psychologist who works with children with LBLDs. Reading specialists, learning specialists, and educational consultants might also be helpful. There are a number of credible organizations that can help you connect with the appropriate specialists in your area; see a list of helpful resources at http://www.newharbinger.com/40989. Regardless of where your referral comes from, carefully vet any specialist or consultant you are considering; see chapter 2 for guidance on how to vet providers.

Step 2: Break the Cycle of Negative Feedback

Most children with LBLDs are caught in an infinite loop of negativity—from peers, teachers, and even family members. Fortunately, you can inject positivity into your child's life, helping him or her develop a positive self-image. Let's hear how Nate reacted to negative comments.

Nate's Story (continued)

One day, Nate's nanny peered into Nate's room and saw that he was reluctant to get started on the work I had set out for him. Upset by this, she said, "That's it, Nate. You're not doing your work so you've lost your playtime." She did not understand that when Nate was behaving this way, it was not just willful defiance; schoolwork was so packed with strong, negative feelings for him that it was a truly painful experience. Nate knew he should be working, but he couldn't.

I later learned that Nate's teachers often complained about Nate's "poor" writing and his inability to pass tests, which were sometimes composed entirely of essay questions that he could not answer, precisely because of those "poor" written language skills. The result? Failing grades for Nate, which were closely *accompanied by an ugly subtext that was clear to him, his parents, and me: This child isn't good enough for this school. He doesn't belong here.*

It is understandable why Nate felt that there was something wrong with him, and it is not surprising that he often became upset at the very mention of homework.

Identify people who promote a positive self-image for your child. Find ways to incorporate these people into your child's life. They could be relatives, family friends, an art or music teacher, or a sports coach. At the same time, move away from individuals who diminish your child's self-image. It might not always be obvious, but there could be some people whose interactions with your child result in elevated anxiety, low self-esteem, and negative self-image.

Collaborate with others to plan a positive learning experience for your child. Help your child's teachers and school administrators develop a positive mindset about your child by demonstrating the effort you and your child are making. Convene a meeting with your child's teachers. At the meeting, share your observations about your child's experiences and ask what they have observed. Work together to set priorities for supporting your child at home and at school. Create a plan that takes into account your child's unique learning, social, and emotional needs. Collectively determine how and when you will meet again to assess progress and adjust support. If your relationship with your child's teacher has been strained, identify another individual at your child's school who can help you advocate for your son or daughter. Bring your concerns to the attention of this individual. Once you feel you have a good relationship with this person, seek his or her advice on how to best reach out to the teacher or administrators at your child's school.

Step 3: Promote Emotional Regulation

When your child was a toddler, you may have used *redirecting* as a way to prevent a tantrum or calm a crying spell. Maybe you played peek-a-boo or introduced a beloved toy or carried your child to a different environment. While those methods may no longer work for your older child, the idea is the same: sense the approaching emotional struggle and be a comforting resource.

Nate's Story (continued)

As I pieced together the full picture of Nate's home and school experiences, it became apparent that without a healthier emotional life, there would be no way for Nate to thrive. As I got to know Nate better, I could recognize when his anxiety was increasing. Sometimes, I could divert his attention or reassure him before he fell apart. Other times, Nate's anxiety increased so quickly that I could do nothing but watch and, after some time, pick up the pieces.

Sometimes during these outbursts, I would pull one of Nate's favorite books off a shelf and flip through it. Eventually he'd notice, and when he had calmed down a bit, he would come over to join me. Books that were of high interest to him distracted Nate from his troubling thoughts. My looking at his books also signaled that what was of interest to Nate was of interest to me. Nate soon learned that no matter how out of control things became, I would remain calm and connected to him. And once he calmed, we would make a decision, together, about what to do next. Sometimes we'd stop for the day. Often we worked a little bit more. It was important that I was willing to accept either outcome.

Your child will, without a doubt, become upset while you're working together. Here are some important tips to help you be a stabilizing, open, and compassionate parent.

Be calm and patient. Being with a child who is in an agitated state can be an uncomfortable experience; our instinct is to fix what is broken as quickly as possible. But some things can't be rushed. In fact, there is very little we can actually do to bring about a rapid change in a child's state of mind.

Help calm your child if he or she is agitated. As long as your child has a safe and secure relationship with you, your attentiveness will help him or her be calm and emotionally regulated. Be sure to adjust your interactions to suit your child's needs when he or she is agitated. Some highly agitated children need an embrace, whereas others need some space.

Use physical proximity to enhance your child's focus. Humans are social creatures, and children in particular require a sense of closeness to adults with whom they feel safe and secure in order to stay focused. Physical proximity helps children better regulate their emotions and is essential for healthy brain development (Hughes 2009). By staying close to your child during homework time, he or she will be more focused and regulated. As your child is working, you can review homework that has been completed or help organize your child's backpack, binders, and study materials. If it's not distracting to your child, you can try engaging in activities of your own, such as getting caught up on emails or reading. The goal is to stay nearby while your child is working.

Model emotional regulation. Adults often become unsettled by a dysregulated child, and when adults display their agitation, children grow even more upset. It's critical for adults to understand that remaining emotionally regulated is an enormously demanding task for a child. Through great, conscious effort, children can remain emotionally regulated at school; the moment they get home, however, they no longer have the mental energy required to regulate. This is why so many children have their meltdowns at home after school. If you remain calm, your child will be better able to calm him- or herself. When you can move forward after a meltdown without expressing judgment or imposing consequences, children are more willing to engage in homework.

Keep It Low and Slow

In my first few years as a middle school teacher, if I felt my class was getting really amped up and frenetic, I would often fall into being reactive: raising my voice, picking up my own tempo in response. By my third year of teaching, I discovered that exactly the opposite is what's indicated in situations like this. Rather than ratcheting up my own behavior when my students got amped up, I began to pull it down: I learned to move slowly, talk as little as possible, keep a benevolent expression on my face, and show my comfort in the situation. As my students began to observe the changes in me, they calmed down and became more regulated. This works as well in the home as it does in the classroom. Keep calm, and your child will eventually follow suit.

Step 4: Embrace the Value of Play

All mammals, especially young ones, engage in play. Play is more than simply something fun for children to do. Play is an essential means by which youngsters develop important skills and regulate their emotions.

Nate's Story (continued)

When I began working with Nate, I introduced him to playing catch with a baseball and glove. We threw underhand for weeks. After he had gotten the hang of it, I told him that I was going to try an overhand throw and that he might need to make some adjustments in order to catch it. I threw the ball, and he caught it. I had created a small challenge for him, and he had met it successfully. Even though it was a minor victory, he saw that something challenging could become fun. We quickly moved from standing twenty feet apart to thirty feet apart, and finally we were tossing balls from as far as fifty feet away from one another. Games of catch gave Nate an opportunity to see for himself that he was coordinated and that he had good balance and a good eye. He was building a self-confidence he had never had.

I often use playing catch as an icebreaker, a study break, or an end-of-session activity. Play by its very nature is highly engaging, therefore promoting neurological activity and brain development. Furthermore, when play involves vigorous physical activity, there are added benefits. It is well established that the increased blood flow to the brain improves memory and many other brain functions. To understand how a child's brain is functioning, observe his or her body. If the child is slumped over or groggy, so is his or her brain. To get the brain moving, get the child moving.

Here are some tips for integrating play periods into your child's day:

Make time to play with your child on a regular basis. It is easy to push aside play to fulfill responsibilities, but regular, relaxed, positive interactions with your child will be invaluable. Allow time for play breaks before, *during*, and/or after homework. This will generate a more positive attitude toward homework.

Use play to calm your child. Engaging in a fun activity is one of the quickest ways to help settle an upset child. Figure out what your child enjoys doing, and freely dial in the activity when you see it is needed to help calm him or her.

Use play to engage. Any time you recognize that something has piqued your child's interest, allow it to guide what you do next. Getting off task in order to allow a student to pursue an interest is a valuable way of promoting perseverance and motivation (Sansone, Thoman, and Fraughton 2015).

Boost your child's confidence with games. Leveraging skills developed during play can help your child build the confidence needed to take on new challenges. Unlike schoolwork, play is not governed by strict rules. It is easy to ratchet up or down the demands of a play activity so that it provides the optimal level of challenge needed to build confidence. It also promotes the idea that challenges are fun. When I worked with Nate, I used our games of catch to provide positive feedback and point out how he was able to rise to a challenge. I'll never forget the smile that came over his face the day I pointed out he was throwing the baseball with such velocity that it was making a popping sound when it struck my glove. You can use the games you play with your child to help him or her appreciate his or her skill development and progress.

Seek out types of play that require teamwork. Many games are about one person competing with another, and the pressure of competition can be hard on some children. Since we know that internal motivation is promoted when two people collaborate on a task (Carr and Walton 2014), try to engage in games that require you working together as a team. When it's time to return to homework, your child can bring a sense of well-being to the task that, just minutes ago, was so objectionable. An added benefit of play is that it generally results in a positive mood. Positive moods appear to be related to elevated levels of brain flexibility, which might promote better learning outcomes (Sanders 2017).

Encourage a sense of autonomy. Allowing a child to decide what to play and when—even if it means playing a game of catch before starting homework instead of afterward—will promote a sense of autonomy. According to motivation expert Daniel Pink, autonomy promotes motivation (2011). You can leverage this newfound motivation to return to schoolwork with heightened vigor.

Share the responsibility. Even in play, things can go wrong. While playing, find ways to turn a negative into a positive. If something gets broken or a house rule is violated, use it as an opportunity to share with your child that the bad things that sometimes occur are not entirely his or her fault. When adults are willing to share responsibility, children are much more likely to feel calm; they are also better able to learn from the experience.

Respond thoughtfully. Children are incredibly self-conscious and are easily embarrassed. Thoughtful responses to both their accomplishments and their mistakes are often the key to translating the overall experience into a positive outcome. It is sometimes better to downplay moments of impulsivity or inappropriate behavior. Children are smart; they know what's going on. Give them a little time, and they will often make the needed adjustment on their own.

Step 5: Adjust Homework and How Much You Help

For many children with LBLDs, their thoughts about school are profoundly negative. The only way to help children revise their thinking is to adapt what they are required to do so that they are not overwhelmed and can be successful.

Nate's Story (continued)

Even as Nate became more emotionally regulated and we made progress on the academic front, Nate would still sometimes cry before beginning his homework. The reason? Schoolwork still exceeded his capacities, and his repeated failures left him believing that every assignment would be impossible.

Nate's negative thoughts were deeply embedded in his mind— and they weren't leaving anytime soon. Because school hadn't gone well in the past, he expected it to always go poorly. Nate's negative thoughts said, "I'm the kid who can't learn anything. I'm the kid who never understands what is going on. I'm the kid who will never be a good student no matter how hard I try." I strove to help Nate develop positive thoughts that said, "You know, when I get the help I need, and things are explained to me, I can really learn! I'm a good learner, and I think I can do well in school!"

I approached Nate's homework with the same strategy, patience, and gentleness that I brought to each game of catch. During the first few months we worked together, Nate did not complete a single homework assignment in its entirety—because I did not ask him to. I tossed him only the amount of work he could successfully handle. I looked at Nate's homework and broke down each assignment into smaller tasks. This made the work easier for him to tackle and created numerous opportunities for success. Every completed step became an opportunity for positive reinforcement. This strategy prevented Nate from becoming overwhelmed, and it gave him the confidence to believe he was capable of more.

Assess your child's homework and his or her ability. Despite what we like to think about how growth and development occur, what we know is that it is rarely a linear process. To figure out how to adjust your child's homework and projects to his ability, ask these questions:

How much help with homework should I provide? This question needs to be asked *every day*, because your child's capacity for completing homework will change every day. Adjusting how much help you provide requires taking the circumstances of the day into account.

Ask yourself: Is my child tired? Am I squeezing in homework before a sports practice or music lesson? Is the assignment for a subject my child enjoys or one with which he or she struggles? Does my child already have the skills needed to complete the assignment or are they still emerging? Let the answers to these questions shape your expectations for how much your child can reasonably contribute and how much support you will need to provide to keep the experience of completing homework a positive one.

How much homework is right for my child? There is no single answer to this question; it changes day to day. On days when your child is capable of doing a lot, have him or her complete a lot. On days when your son or daughter is *not* capable of doing a lot, be happy with what you get. Children are not like adults; they cannot be expected to apply themselves with consistent effort. Completing only a fraction of an assignment may actually be enough for your child. Even assignments that have been modified to address LBLDs can still be overwhelming.

Communicate your willingness to be flexible about homework. It's important that you tell your child that you are willing to adjust your expectations based on the circumstances at hand. When your child knows that you are comfortable with his or her inconsistency, it helps him or her feel safe and comfortable; it also, interestingly enough, helps him or her feel capable of greater effort.

Step 6: Intervene During a Crisis

There *will* be homework emergencies and special projects pushed aside until the last minute. The good news is that there are strategies for handling these crises.

Nate's Story (continued)

One evening after a lengthy homework session, I was packing up my things. Nate was my last of many students that day, and I was ready to get home. As I pulled on my jacket and picked up my briefcase,

Nate stopped me. "Daniel, I also have this." He held out a crumpled sheet of paper. On it were the requirements for a research paper, which was due the next day. I burst out laughing. "Nate," I said, "What in the world? This is due tomorrow."

All of us, and children too, put things off. Unfortunately for children, sometimes the consequences of not completing an assignment can be dire. It's no mystery that a child with an LBLD is not always going to be forthcoming about a difficult assignment like a research paper. These moments can be trying for all parents. They are especially trying for parents of children with LBLDs because they occur with more frequency. Here's what to do:

Provide help! When a homework crisis occurs, the most important lesson your child can learn is that you are a reliable source of support. Children with LBLDs have already had plenty of experience with failure. What they need in the face of a crisis is a sense that things can work out for the better. If your child tells you a big assignment is due the next day, step in and help to the extent it is needed. The goal is to make sure your child's assignment gets done.

Be measured in your response. Find ways to leverage your child's strengths and interests. This strategy will maximize your child's contribution to any homework assignment, but it is critical during a homework emergency. When we are aware of what children are good at and allow them to exercise that capacity, they feel encouraged and are more likely to stay focused on the task at hand. You can further enhance your child's willingness to stay focused by identifying topics that he or she is interested in as the basis of writing assignments and school projects. For example, if your child loves soccer and is required to write a research paper on a country, help your child choose a nation where a famous soccer player plays.

Prioritize your child's emotional regulation over his or her contribution. As you work on a last-minute assignment, your child, out of guilt or shame, might be eager to contribute beyond what he or she reasonably can or, alternatively, might display resistant behavior. Be careful how much work you ask your child to contribute. If you and your child are feeling calm, that is a big accomplishment and promotes a secure bond. Furthermore, your child will only be able to learn if he or she is emotionally regulated. By prioritizing emotional regulation, your child will be able to focus the limited energy he or she has on the academic objectives.

> In the immortal words of Erma Bombeck, "A child needs your love the most when he deserves it least." Need I say more?

Take steps to prevent another homework emergency. Once the crisis is over, take a moment to reflect on what happened. Ask yourself, "What parts of handling the crisis went well? What can we do differently if it happens again? Are there supplies I should keep on hand to be better prepared?" And perhaps most important, "Why were the assignment and its due date revealed on such short notice? What can be done to prevent this from happening again?" I often counsel parents to routinely check in with the teacher about homework assignments. When projects are assigned, break out the steps for your child and create a calendar for completing portions of the assignment. Collaborate with your child as much as needed on each portion until the assignment is complete.

Step 7: Stay Patient and Positive

Struggling children, especially children with LBLDs, are exposed to huge amounts of corrective input from adults. It's very important to make sure this feedback is not shaming, particularly when your child feels that he or she has failed.

Nate's Story (continued)

Over time, Nate began to invest more and more energy into his schoolwork. I remember the first time he actually studied for a test. It was a science test, and he wanted to start studying for it the day he learned about it. This was momentous in and of itself.

*We had about a week to study. Every day, Nate spent hours
trying to memorize science vocabulary and learn scientific concepts.
It was hard, but he was determined, and he worked as diligently as
I had ever seen him. But in the end, he got a D on the test for which
he'd studied so hard.*

It's a pattern I see all the time: after a tremendous investment of
time and energy, the initial attempts do not always result in high marks.
Adults need to be very careful about how we respond to these nascent
efforts, even if (or especially when) they don't result in good grades. Here
are ways to proactively respond:

Accept that progress will be slow. Always keep in mind that progress
is not linear, especially for a child with an LBLD. Progress is often said
to be two steps forward and one step back. It is simply not realistic to
expect equal improvement across several categories at the same rate.

Value responsibilities over results. Place a greater stock in your child
being a responsible student than in getting good grades, especially during
his or her early efforts. Being a responsible student means giving consistent effort, finishing assignments, turning in assignments on time, and
studying for tests. If your child is consistently working to understand his
or her academic material and is given appropriate opportunities to
demonstrate his or her knowledge, the grades will eventually follow.

Avoid using reward systems. It has been my experience that reward
systems frequently backfire. A child may become so preoccupied with
the reward that he or she is unable to engage meaningfully in the task set
out before him or her. In addition, a withheld reward, in the eyes of a
child, can feel like a punishment (Kohn 1999). Focus instead on the
internal reward both you and your child will experience through a
successful collaboration. Engage in activities that honor your relationship and are done regardless of school going well. Such unconditional
rewards are an effective means of maintaining positivity over time, no
matter what.

Prioritize collaboration. As I've noted earlier, working—and playing—
together reaps countless benefits. Indeed, prioritizing the value of effort

and collaboration over other considerations promotes a growth mindset and further learning (Dweck 2007). Nothing feels more rewarding than having worked hard toward a goal together and having achieved it, especially when it's done in the context of a healthy positive relationship. When your child is struggling, build in some quality time together—these experiences are frequently the basis for a lasting healthy connection.

Respect your child. Be aware of what your child is really capable of doing, and do not force him or her to do something that will exceed his or her capacities. By treating your child with respect and injecting positivity into his or her life, you will be tilling the ground for positive learning experiences and overall progress.

Nate's Story (continued)

Establishing a positive collaboration with Nate took a long time. It took him time to develop the skills that were emerging slowly. It took him time to learn that he was capable and clever. But by the time Nate reached high school, he was happily anticipating going to college, which he did—and it was a privilege for me to see. Watching Nate over the years taught me that a positive relationship can change a child's life. And when he graduated from high school, I gave Nate the baseball glove he'd used every time we played catch—just to remind him how far he'd come.

Conclusion

For a child, the trauma of doing poorly at school frequently results in the formation of negative thoughts that can be deep and lasting. If left unchanged, a negative self-image can detrimentally impact a child's life well beyond school. A critical step in bringing about positive change for your child and you in the face of school-related trauma is working together in a highly collaborative way. The awareness that your child can be successful when working collaboratively with you is itself positive thinking.

With the right help, at the right time, and in the right amount, all children can experience tremendous success at school and in life. Keep in mind these key steps designed to help you and your child heal through positive change:

Step 1. Identify the problem

Step 2. Break the cycle of negative feedback

Step 3. Promote emotional regulation

Step 4. Embrace the value of play

Step 5. Adjust homework and how much you help

Step 6. Intervene during a crisis

Step 7. Stay patient and positive

CHAPTER 5

Navigating School

Navigating school isn't easy for children with LBLDs, and it can be challenging for parents, too. If, however, you build partnerships with your child's teachers and school administrators, anticipate when your child will need extra help, and take proactive measures to provide help, both you and your child will be able to successfully navigate school. Special-education expert Richard Lavoie describes this process as "preparing your child for school and preparing the school for your child."

In this chapter, you'll learn strategies for building partnerships with school faculty as well as how to help your child engage in the classroom and prepare for tests and quizzes at home. You'll explore how you can mitigate the challenges that you and your child are most likely to encounter. Finally, you'll also learn to recognize when it might be time to seek the support of a tutor.

Establishing Good Relationships with Teachers and Administrators

Some years, your child will have a teacher who is a perfect match for his or her learning needs. Other years, the match might not be as good. As a parent, your job is to forge a positive working relationship with every teacher your child has. This encourages teachers and school administrators to recognize and accommodate your child's unique learning needs; they'll also come to view your child in the most positive light possible. This will improve your child's self-esteem and interest in learning. Additionally, by building these working relationships in a professional manner, you'll model professionalism for your child.

The strategies I share in this chapter foster an approach to working with your child's teachers and administrators that is based on kindness.

Initiating Communication

Schedule a meeting at the start of the school year or as soon as you learn who your child's teacher will be. The first meeting sets the groundwork for the entire school year. Let the teacher know your child loves learning but may need extra help. Tell the teacher that you will do all you can to provide whatever support he or she recommends. If you are already working with school administrators, you can ask if they should be included in this meeting.

Include homework in your conversation. It is important to understand a teacher's expectations for the coming year so that you can help complete assignments correctly. For example, some teachers only want to see that an attempt was made on an assignment while others expect proofread submissions. You should also collaborate with your child's teacher regarding a plan for when your child does not understand a concept or cannot complete an assignment.

Finally, ask about the length of time the teacher expects students to spend on homework. Follow up with: "What happens if my child frequently needs to spend a significantly longer amount of time on homework? Are there adjustments that can be made so that homework takes a similar amount of time as it does for the rest of the class? Can my child receive extensions?" By seeking answers to these questions, you will be able to help your child have a successful start to the school year.

Maintaining Communication

Ask your child's teacher how he or she prefers to communicate and when. It is also good to ask about a reasonable timeframe to receive a response. Respect the teacher's boundaries, and don't expect responses on weekends or in the evenings. A good way to approach this is to ask, "When would it be okay for me to follow up?"

If you are concerned about an issue, request a meeting. It's tempting to pop in or start chatting after school, but it's not the best strategy. You deserve to have an uninterrupted conversation, and your child's teacher deserves time to set up a game plan for fully addressing your concerns. If you choose to start an impromptu conversation, however, at least begin by asking if it's okay to start the conversation and offering to schedule a different time, if needed.

You will maximize meetings with your child's teacher if you come prepared, encourage him or her to speak freely, and work together to come up with steps that can be taken in the classroom and reinforced at home. End your meetings by setting a date to check in or meet again so that you leave with a plan for the moment and a timeframe for next steps. Send a follow-up email summarizing the main conclusions to confirm your understanding and the tasks ahead. Be sure to express gratitude for all attendees' time and caring.

End-of-the-Year Meetings and Summer Academics

The focus of an end-of-the-year meeting should be to create a summer plan for academic support and to prepare your child for the transition into the next school year. Schedule the meeting so that your child's teacher and others involved have plenty of time to put together a plan of action before school lets out. Four to five weeks ahead of time is a good aim. For a template of what to write in an outreach letter, please see the downloadable sample letter at http://www.newharbinger.com/40989.

While you're planning ahead for summer and even the start of the next school year, it's also wise to think about helping your child make a smooth transition. Children with LBLDs often struggle with transitioning from period to period, day to day, and even semester to semester. Visit this book's website, http://www.newharbinger.com/40989, for tips on how you can ease these transitions for your son or daughter.

Troubleshooting at School Meetings

Teachers, administrators, and family members all view your child through different lenses. The combination of your collective efforts should bring both challenges and solutions into focus. Even under the best of circumstances, however, you can still hit a bump in the road. If you feel that something is not going well and would like to schedule a meeting to seek a resolution, try these strategies:

- **Begin your conversation with a positive.** Point out something that has gone well for your child in the classroom or at school, or something that your child has particularly enjoyed learning.

- **Collect information.** Even if you believe you know what the issue is and why it is happening—and even if you have a suggestion for its remedy—it's wise to ask your child's teacher for his or her perspective *first*. Ask what he or she thinks some of your child's difficulties might be. When the teacher believes that he or she can speak openly, he or she is then able to be in a thoughtful state and offer a helpful strategy.

- **Share child-initiated solutions.** If you are brought in to discuss your child's inappropriate behavior, come to the meeting prepared. First, know that it is easy for a child with LBLDs to become overwhelmed—and when your child feels overwhelmed, he or she may exhibit challenging behavior. Second, try engaging your child in a conversation about what happened and why it is problematic. After listening, help your child accept responsibility for his or her actions, and work together to identify the root of the problem. Third, take measures that prevent your child from feeling overwhelmed again. Ask your child to offer ideas about other, better ways he or she can initiate and respond to similar interactions. Help your son or daughter refine the proposed approach and make suggestions to improve it. Finally, share with your child's teachers and administrators what you and your child discussed and what the plan is to avoid future incidents.

- **Suggest a seat assignment.** If you have a sense of what desk location is optimal for your child, you might share your observation with the teacher. This also goes for personal space in general. If you believe that the teacher's moving closer to or farther away from your child may help him or her stay in a more regulated state, speak up.

- **Politely ask for a reason.** On extremely rare occasions, I have encountered teachers and administrators who appeared unable to view children I've worked with in a positive light. These moments are devastating to parents and children. It will be difficult for you to not feel defensive if a teacher or administrator says, "He's just lazy" or "He's being manipulative." I recommend your only response be, "Why do you think that might be?" If there is another equally thin response, such as "He doesn't seem to care," refrain from saying anything other than repeating the same question, "Why do you think that might be?" You will best be able to defend your child if you assist teachers and administrators through this investigative process, even if it may be more labor intensive.

Now that we've explored steps you can take to communicate with your child's teacher, let's explore how else you can help your child be successful in the classroom.

Establishing Good Habits in the Classroom

As a parent of a child with a language-based learning disability, you need to be vigilant regarding all of the demands that will be placed on your child from the moment he or she starts school. Fulfilling these demands requires a dizzying number of skills, many of which are probably slowly emerging in your child. To help your child get through each school day, you'll want to model and support good habits in the areas of communication, self-advocacy, and organization.

Communication Skills

You can help your child build communication skills by anticipating what he or she might be required to communicate during the school day, and then helping him or her prepare for these encounters.

Role playing—which can be done almost anywhere, at any time, and cover any situation your child might encounter—is a great way to practice different likely scenarios. Have your child take turns in each role to practice initiating and responding. The more you practice with your child, the more skillful and confident your child will be. Additionally, it will offer further insight into the conversations your child is having at school.

You can also help your son or daughter create nonverbal cues or hand gestures to use with teachers. Children tend to feel less anxious when they have signals that indicate their discomfort and that prompt an adult into supportive action. The adults working with your child also might appreciate using a nonverbal reminder to curtail a recurring behavior. To be effective, the gesture should be simple and specific. For example, moving hands apart can remind a child to step back and reestablish personal space, or a finger on the lips can remind a child to not interrupt. Make sure your child understands the gesture and its meaning, and has a chance to practice responding to it. Also, it's often overwhelming to implement a series of gestures at the same time. Focus on one or two important signals before adding additional cues.

Self-Advocacy Skills

All parents want their children to be able to speak up for themselves at school. Children who are able to do so can identify and articulate what they need. But for children with LBLDs, self-advocacy emerges slowly. This is due in part to the fact that speaking up for oneself is the end result of mastering *many* skills, including effective communication, self-awareness, and the ability to plan and initiate.

With your help, your child can learn how to express his or her needs. This ability comes in handy in all sorts of situations, but particularly when he or she doesn't understand a concept well enough to complete an assignment or study for a test. Here are ways you can assist:

- Help your child come up with questions to ask his or her teacher.

- Act as your child's scribe by writing down his or her questions.

- Help your child figure out when to meet with the teacher.

- If your child's teacher prefers email, help your child draft an email.

- Demonstrate ways your child can be respectful so that he or she can build a good working relationship with the teacher.

When your child plans to speak with a teacher, follow up with him or her by asking what happened. If your child didn't speak with the teacher, provide specific prompts. For example, encourage your child to speak with the teacher before class starts, or at the end of class, or during recess. If your child still didn't speak with the teacher after being prompted, become your child's safety net—help your son or daughter draft an email to the teacher either asking the questions or requesting a meeting to do so.

Organizational Skills

If your child has a difficult time staying organized, implement steps to scaffold organization at school until your child has the confidence and skillset to do so independently. In elementary school, this may mean that you check your child's desk weekly to stay on top of the materials and assignments your child is given. Try to do this when few students will be around to minimize any potential embarrassment for your child.

Take a proactive role in organizing your child's backpack and folders. If your child's teacher maintains a website with assignments and test dates, check the site daily. If assignments are only posted in the classroom, request permission to take pictures at pick-up or drop-off, or request that your child be allowed to do so at a time that will not disrupt the class. In the upper grades, when your child is assigned a locker, you should check it weekly.

Reconsidering How You Value Grades and Independent Learning

The first priority at school should always be learning. Yet adults and children have been primed to aim not for mastery of subjects but to get golden stars and the highest grades, and to do so without any help. As you well know, this can be virtually impossible for a child with an LBLD. I suggest that you reconsider the value you—and your child—place on grades and being an independent learner.

Support vs. Independence

It is more important to prevent a gap in your child's knowledge from widening than it is to force his or her independence. Your child's capacity for reaching out to his or her teacher independently will come in time with practice, skill development, and confidence.

As discussed in chapter 3, it's important to recognize that a secure, healthy, positive relationship with your child is what promotes independence. When your child believes that you are a safe and reliable source of support, he or she will have the capacity to explore and grow. Withholding support will make your child more dependent on you. Children who are forced to sink or swim rarely learn to swim. Worse still, they come to see the person who threw them in as untrustworthy.

I am often asked, "What happens if my child isn't allowed to fail? How will he or she learn?" I understand that we learn by picking up the pieces after making a mistake; however, children with language-based learning difficulties often feel like they are *always* making mistakes at school. We can only learn from failure when almost everything else in our lives is going right. Otherwise, we are just experiencing failure after failure and compounding the damage to our self-esteem. *There is absolutely no benefit to allowing a child to constantly fail.* The journey is hard enough. What a struggling child needs is support, so he or she can begin to experience some success.

Academic Responsibility vs. Grades

All children learn early on that their value as a student is measured by the grades they get. For children with LBLDs, achieving good grades is very difficult. Help your child develop a healthy perspective about grades by focusing instead on being a responsible student. Being a responsible student means applying consistent effort, completing assignments, submitting assignments on time, and preparing for tests. When your child achieves these things, and is rewarded for it, the grades he or she gets will have less significance. Your child will need your help to fulfill these responsibilities, but the effort will be worthwhile for both you and your child.

You will also need to help your child understand that the priority is to learn the material, not to get a specific grade. That said, when energy is focused on fulfilling your child's academic responsibilities as a team, grades will improve.

•   Andy's Story

I worked with an eighth-grader named Andy who, after months of resisting homework, finally began making an effort to study for a science test. For the first time, he studied diligently for many hours over the course of several days, attempting to learn the material. He was eager to show his teacher what he had learned. But despite his efforts, he bombed the test.

When I arrived for my session with Andy, I was met by a glum young man who held up his science test with a big red "F" on it. I rewrote the grade on his paper to reflect the "A" I felt he earned for effort. I also helped him understand that his efforts weren't in vain. I used this opportunity to recognize his hard work, reminding him of all of the things he did to prepare for the test. I let him know that working in this way would, eventually, translate into better grades.

Even though it is difficult for children with LBLDs to get good grades, and it's important to emphasize responsibility over results, children do benefit from good grades, especially in terms of self-esteem. That's why I encourage you to provide as much support as your child needs. One of the best ways to promote learning and improve your child's grades is to help him or her become an active learner and a skilled test taker.

Strategies for Promoting Active Learning

Active learning is engaging in content thoughtfully and interactively. Students who think deeply about what is being taught, actively engage in discussions, and ask questions learn significantly more than students who are passive. Fortunately, there are a number of things you can do to help your child become an active learner:

Pre-teach subjects. Through communication with your child's teacher and by carefully reviewing the class website, you can be apprised of content that will be taught in class. Then you can teach one or two concepts to your child *ahead of time*. This will allow your child to better follow class conversation, stay engaged, and contribute. Not only does this approach promote better attention, but it also boosts comprehension.

Encourage physical adjustments. Ask your child to sit up straight during class. This improves attention and breathing, increasing oxygen flow to the brain. Also, encourage your child to follow the teacher with his or her eyes. This enhances engagement and signals to the teacher that your child is paying attention.

Encourage asking questions. During homework sessions, help your child prepare questions to ask while in class. Encourage your child to ask at least one question every day. Explain that asking questions is one way teachers recognize participation. If your child isn't comfortable asking questions during class, urge your child to ask questions during the teacher's "office hours," which are typically before or after school, during lunch, or during a free period.

Encourage class participation. Contributing to class discussions is another way a teacher recognizes participation. Help your child research class topics, then encourage him or her to introduce new or additional information to the class discussion.

Encourage active listening. This means that your child should periodically ask him- or herself, "What am I listening for? Do I understand what I am hearing? What words are new to me? Even if I don't ask, what questions could I ask if I wanted to?" Help your child determine when listening will be more effective than taking notes. If taking notes makes it difficult to understand what is being said, your child should focus on listening instead. Your child can always write down what he or she remembers **after** the lecture. If this is not feasible, you can offer to take notes for your child based on what he or she remembers from class.

Tips for Promoting Note Taking Skills

If your child can handle listening and taking notes at the same time, urge him or her to do so. Remind your child that note taking does not have to be a verbatim recording.

First, help your child **prepare** to take notes by dedicating space in his or her binder or notebook. Provide prompts on the paper, such as numbering 1 to 10. Encourage your child, even if he or she is reluctant, to write down a few of the important words he or she hears during a presentation. Doing this will encourage eventual note taking and increase the likelihood that your child will be able to recall what was heard.

If your child has difficulty writing while listening, teach him or her to write three or four key words or concepts he or she remembers **after** class. You can also invite your child to draw pictures or diagrams instead of writing words. At home, review the notes your child has taken. Make sure the class date has been recorded, and fill in information your child may have missed using textbooks, the Internet, or a classmate's notes. Make sure the notes are filed neatly so that they can be used for future studying.

Tips for Promoting Test Taking Skills

Another key to both learning and achieving good grades is effective studying and test preparation. When approached strategically, test and quiz preparation can be the most effective means of filling in the gaps your child may have in content knowledge. The ability to prepare effectively for tests will also help your child for years to come.

• *Marco's Story*

Years ago, I worked with an upper-elementary school student who was failing across the board. I began providing remedial instruction and reviewing the concepts Marco was taught each day. Soon enough, I learned he had an upcoming social studies test. As I began to draft a study calendar, I asked him what would be covered on the test. Marco said, "It's a test! You never know what's going to be on it. That's why it's called a test!"

Marco believed that all test material was a complete mystery. This is not uncommon. Many children need help understanding that while they may not know the exact questions that will be on a test, they should have a clear understanding of which concepts will be covered. It is your job as a parent and study partner to help your child identify when tests will be given, what will be on the tests, and how to adequately prepare for them.

Familiarize yourself with the material. To help your child study for a specific test, you will need to know what material will be covered and create a reasonable study plan. This might entail touching base with the teacher, organizing notes, creating summaries of the material, and establishing a study calendar.

Create a thinking map. A *thinking map* is a visual representation of abstract thoughts. These and other graphic organizers can be filled in while reading to help your child organize key information and see relationships. Thinking maps can look like a tree, a spider web, a train—anything your child has an interest in that has interconnecting parts, which illustrates connectivity of concepts. These drawings enhance the brain's natural ability to detect and construct patterns, and they reduce anxiety by providing familiar visual patterns for organizing one's thoughts. Sometimes teachers provide these, or you can find them online with the search terms "thinking map."

Prepare for in-class essays. To prepare for in-class essays, you can help your child anticipate what the essay questions might be. Engage your child in a conversation about how these questions might be answered. Then record his or her ideas, and remind your child of any important concepts or connections. You may even need to write out entire essays to the possible test questions with your child.

Ensure your child gets enough sleep. Being well rested also plays a role in how well your child is able to perform on tests. You may be able to encourage your child to get more sleep by explaining that even though the brain only occupies 3 percent of body mass, it consumes 25 to 30 percent of all calories. Therefore, the brain needs to be given the chance to rest in order to store information as efficiently as possible. To help your child fall asleep more easily—and to sleep better through the night—set a rule to turn off all electronics one hour before going to bed.

Promote strategies that improve test performance. Before answering any test questions, have your son or daughter cue his or her memory by immediately writing down formulas and key words. Also, get your child in the habit of previewing the test before answering anything. Have your child read the directions twice. Then answer the easy questions first. Encourage your child to ask for clarification from the teacher any time he or she is the least bit uncertain about the directions. Teachers appreciate seeing effort, even if the answer is incorrect, so encourage your child to answer every question, even if it is just one word or sentence. Your child may be awarded partial credit.

Review tests once they have been graded. This practice helps your child master material and prepare for future cumulative tests. It also reinforces the idea that learning the material is more important than whatever score was received. Begin reviewing together by noting what went well. Then look at any mistakes and determine which answer would have been correct and why. If the correct answer is unclear, and sometimes it is, help your child reach out to his or her teacher for clarification. If your child receives a low grade and wants to seek options for grade recovery, help him or her ask the teacher whether it is possible to retake the test or be given an additional assignment. If grade recovery isn't an option, don't worry. Focus on helping your child learn the material and prepare for the next assignment or test.

By approaching studying as a joint effort, you maximize your child's ability to learn and retrieve information. For handy checklists you can print and refer to while collaborating with your child, refer to the Test Preparation Checklist and the Test Taking Tips resources on this book's website: http://www.newharbinger.com/40989.

Tips to Ease Test Anxiety

Test anxiety is a common occurrence, especially for children with LBLDs. You can help reduce your child's anxiety about upcoming tests by helping your son or daughter prepare and practice as much as possible. Help your child keep things in perspective by reminding him or her that "It's just a test. In the grand scheme of things, you will do well in life."

Sian Beilock's *Choke* (2011) offers a good pretest writing exercise designed to reduce test-taking anxiety. Here's what she recommends: Engage in a discussion with your child prior to the exam. You might say, "Tell me what your biggest concerns are." After your child answers, you can say, "You're right. Time is a consideration." Or "Oh, that is a valid concern." Or "You have been studying very hard. You have a lot to be proud of already."

Finally, by encouraging your child to use specific strategies during test time, as noted above, anxiety can be greatly reduced. Your child will feel prepared and confident if he or she has a routine that'll help him or her remember what he or she studied.

Knowing When to Bring in a Tutor

As a parent, you are in the best position to know what type of support your child needs. But when your child is learning a subject that is difficult for you to learn and explain, or when working on homework together creates far more tension than it provides support, it's time to consider outsourcing help.

Choose a tutor who is a good personality match for your child and someone who has an awareness of your child's learning and behavioral characteristics. The experience and expertise of tutors vary enormously, as do their rates. When choosing a tutor, vet him or her carefully. Seek a recommendation from a trusted friend or school personnel. Vetting could include requesting college transcripts, getting a background check, checking references, and conducting an interview.

Spend your money wisely. Bringing a tutor on board can rapidly turn into a significant investment; however, infrequent sessions can be ineffective and possibly wasteful. Unless your child only needs help reviewing for a test or proofreading a paper, effective support requires frequency and consistency.

Clearly state your goals. Share effective strategies, and work with the tutor to structure sessions in a way that addresses the most significant issues. Think of the tutor as your partner, but also allow your child and the tutor a certain degree of autonomy. In general, sessions will be more effective when your child and tutor are able to forge a healthy bond and approach the demands of schoolwork as a team.

Conclusion

Helping your child navigate school involves a high degree of thoughtfulness, planning, effort, follow through, and patience. You will need to be proactive and to unashamedly micromanage your child to help him or her cope with the many demands of schoolwork. Your efforts will boost your child's learning, skill development, and, ultimately, independence.

In this day and age, all parents have become sensitive to providing high levels of support. Indeed, the "helicopter" parent has become one of the most feared designations. As long as your efforts are specifically intended to help your child develop socially, emotionally, and academically, you deserve to be proud of the parent you are.

CHAPTER 6

Dyslexia: Unable to Read in a Reading World

Few learning disabilities have a more widespread impact on a child than dyslexia. Dyslexia affects all written language skills in addition to some areas of short-term memory, sequencing, listening comprehension, and expressive language. Yet prior to entering school, children with dyslexia generally appear quite normal relative to other children. When they begin school, however, they quickly learn that they are different from their peers, and they often come to believe they are not as capable of learning. Negative thoughts form quickly and, if not addressed properly, can have far-reaching consequences. Fortunately, you are optimally positioned to support your child in ways that will allow him or her to excel not only with written language but also with learning in general.

Early identification and intervention are essential to minimize the impact a reading disability can have on your child. If you recognize that your child is struggling with written language skills, no matter how old he or she is, you should intervene as soon as possible. It never hurts to seek the expertise of a reading specialist; his or her analysis might end up being incredibly helpful.

But you do not need extensive training or sophisticated instructional materials to provide your child with excellent reading support. In fact, you, as the parent of a child with slowly emerging reading skills, can prevent him or her from falling behind at school more easily than you think. In this chapter, you will learn how to create a culture of language in your home, provide hands-on reading instruction, and improve your child's vocabulary.

Creating a Culture of Language in Your Home

The first step in promoting written language skills is providing children a language-rich environment. This is an environment in which parents and other adults actively engage in verbal communication with the child from birth. Engaging all children in verbal communication is critical; it is especially so for children with dyslexia, because it helps them accurately recognize the sounds of words and become familiar with rhythm, rhyme, and cadence, which characterize written and spoken language. Spoken language skills will also help children with dyslexia develop the bypass strategies (see chapter 3 for a refresher) necessary to navigate terrain dense with written language.

Even the youngest child benefits from engaging in fun games of mimicking silly sounds and made-up speech. These games are most effective when the demands are kept well within the capacities of the child so that he or she succeeds and feels rewarded by the play. You'll know what's working by observing your child's response. Stay attuned, pay attention, and let your child teach *you* what he or she needs most when it comes to developing spoken language. The two of you will have enormous success and fun with this kind of play. Play, after all, is nature's best teaching tool, not only when learning to speak and listen but also when learning to read and write.

Following rich spoken language exposure, the next step is to read to your child daily. For a child with dyslexia, being read to is especially important because it may be the only way he or she will gain exposure to print, albeit indirectly. Even as children get older, hearing written language read aloud gives children with dyslexia the opportunity to recognize written language, which differs from spoken language in a number of significant ways. For example, spoken language tends to be more casual and does not always adhere to the same structure and rules of written language. Hearing written language helps children with dyslexia develop an ear for the structure and rules of written language.

Parents should aim to spend twenty minutes a day reading to or with their children. However, keep in mind that *the quality of the interaction you have with your child while reading is more important than the length of time you spend reading.* It's better to read for only five minutes or skip reading altogether if it causes conflict between you and your child. Keep in mind that your child's frustration threshold for reading will change frequently. That's to be expected.

The strategies that follow are designed to help you thoughtfully tailor your approach to your child's needs. Paying close attention to how your child responds to a strategy will help you gauge whether you should keep using that strategy or move on to another; it will also be your guide to how much reading your child is capable of doing on the day and even hour that you work together. Additionally, paying close attention to your child allows you to see he or she *is* learning. You will become aware of what skills your child has mastered and where he or she needs further assistance.

Create a calm space to read. Make sure there are few distractions, ample light, and comfortable seating.

Consider the distance between you and your child. Ask your child what seating arrangement he or she would like while you read together. Your child may prefer to be sitting on your lap or seated nearby. When your child begins to do some of the reading, you might consider increasing the distance between the two of you. Many children are distracted when they feel their parents are looking over their shoulder as they read. Sometimes, I close my eyes and rest my head on my hand to let the child know I'm enjoying being read to. I'll occasionally say words of encouragement to let the child know I'm listening—you can do the same.

Select reading material your child will enjoy. Children don't choose to read a book based on its reading level. They choose it because it's interesting or because it's what their friends are reading. Your job is to help your child feel good about whatever it is that he or she wants to read. If your child chooses easier material, avoid making any comments about how easy it is; a child may take such comments to mean that you don't value his or her efforts or preferences. If your child likes to read the same book over and over, that's okay too.

Make the book relevant to your child. No matter what you're reading together, find a way to express enjoyment, even if you find the material dry. Your enthusiasm will help your child find something relatable in the reading activity. If you need additional help to make the text meaningful, find film footage of the characters or events. If your child is assigned a novel, help him or her understand who the author is, perhaps even something the author and your child have in common.

Keep reading-together time fun. No matter who is reading, make sure your child enjoys the experience! This may mean that you do all of the reading until your child is eager to read a word or two, perhaps even a sentence. It's far better to read to your child than to have him or her anxious and resistant about having to read aloud. A day may come when your child wants to read aloud. That's great! But if he or she decides the following day not to read, that's okay. Do not force your child to read aloud.

Consider pointing out words. Some children like when you point to each word as you read; others don't. Ask your child what he or she prefers. It can also be helpful to hold a blue index card under the sentence being read. I have found that blue cards work best because they contrast with the white of the page, and eyes adjust easily to blue. This makes it easier for children to follow along while you read, or for them to stay focused while they read on their own.

A Few Thoughts on E-Readers

Many parents enjoy using electronic devices that read books aloud. There are a number of benefits of e-readers, including easing the demands of reading together and increasing the exposure a child has to oral reading. In my opinion, however, there is no substitute for a parent doing the reading to his or her child. Why? Because a child perceives the parent's act of reading as a gesture of love and compassion. The extra effort on the part of the parent, especially when the reading is done in a playful and theatrical way, is sure to warm a child's heart and allow him or her to feel closer to his or her parent.

Try articles. Reading an article from a magazine or website can be very fun for middle and high schoolers. Though the articles may contain unfamiliar words or subject matter, children will really work at understanding a piece if they are truly interested in it. The best thing about magazine articles is that they are usually not very long, so even if a child only reads a few paragraphs, he or she will have read a significant amount of the article.

Be a model reader. The late child therapist Edith Sullwold said, "Children do not listen to what we say. They listen to who we are." In short, being a model reader will make reading a habit for your child. If your child sees you reading in your free time, he or she will be more motivated to read in his or her free time; your interest in reading will spark your child's interest. Take regular trips to the library, browse bookstores, and fill your home with a wide array of texts. In addition, you can model *skilled reading*. Think out loud: "Okay, what do I want to learn from this page?" "Oh, I see there's an unusual word that appears several times on this page. I think it would be a good idea for me to figure out what it means before reading further." "This story reminds me of a book I once read. In that book, two enemies ended up being best friends. I wonder if that will happen in this story too."

How to Correct Reading Mistakes

Your child is bound to stumble on words. The key to correcting a child's mistakes is to use a thoughtful approach that offers assistance rather than critique. If your child has chosen to read aloud, you should begin by saying, "If you come to a word you don't know, let me know if you want me to help. Otherwise, I'm going to just listen."

If your child gets stuck, be patient. Wait for at least ten seconds. Though it will feel long, waiting patiently will teach your child that you are going to give him or her all the time needed to figure out a challenging word. Your doing nothing allows your child to control the situation. Of course, if your child becomes agitated, ask if he or she would like a little help with the word. But don't jump in without asking your child if that's what he or she wants. If your child asks what the word is, tell him or her. Do not ask your child to sound out a word unless he or she starts sounding it out on his or her own. Your goal is to make the process of reading together as comfortable for your child as possible. Similarly, if your child asks the meaning of a word, you can ask if he or she wants to guess using context clues or just be given the definition. Follow your child's preference. It is important to avoid disrupting the rhythm and experience of your reading-together time.

When your child mispronounces a word, do not correct him or her right away unless the mispronunciation significantly changes the meaning of the sentence. Make a mental note of the word that was misread. When your child comes to a natural pause, like at the end of a paragraph or chapter, go back, point to the word, and ask him or her to read it again. If your child is still unable to read the word correctly, provide the correct pronunciation. Add that word to an index card (later in this chapter you will learn how to use index cards to promote reading skills and memory).

How to Encourage a Reluctant Reader

As you build a routine of reading aloud with your child every day, you may find that you are doing all of the reading, or that your child will read aloud some days and not others. That's okay. When beginning to read, your child may realize that he or she is not yet a good reader. As this realization sinks in, your child may become discouraged.

•   *Elliott's Story*

One day, I arrived at Elliott's house. I was met by his mother, and she had a concerned look. Elliott was sitting on his bed crying. I sat down in his desk chair. We didn't talk; we just looked out the window together. Finally, Elliott turned to me and said, "I'm dumb. I'm never going to learn to read." I told him that I knew it was hard, but that he was already learning. He didn't respond.

I sat for a moment and noticed a tree in the front yard. I asked, "Is that tree growing?" He said yes. "Can you see it grow?" I asked. He shook his head no. I said, "For some of us, learning to read is slow, like how a tree grows. We can't really tell we're learning and growing. But trees do grow, and you are learning to read."

Elliott enjoyed analogies, and I could tell that he appreciated the comparison. He and I started up again, slowly at first. The changes didn't happen overnight, but, a few months later, he began to pick up momentum. I had begun reading The Little Prince *to him. He was fascinated by this curious story. We were about halfway through the book when I asked if he wanted to read a little bit. He agreed. Page by page, we completed the book. When we finished, he asked if we could read it again, and we did, at a brisker pace.*

Instead of drawing attention to your child's reluctance to read with you or to read aloud, be patient and encourage his or her engagement. You want your child to feel as comfortable as possible with the entire process of reading. Start with favorite books or magazines that your child has already read. After you have read for a while, see if your child is willing to take a turn with a word, sentence, paragraph, or page. Slowly build up the amount your child reads aloud.

You can also try a new book on one of your child's favorite subjects. To build familiarity, try reading a page first and then asking if your child will read a sentence or paragraph from the page you have just read.

Children are often motivated to read their own writing. Try writing down your child's thoughts or a story he or she tells you. It's helpful for children to see their ideas in print because it builds familiarity with printed words. When you're transcribing your child's words, go easy on correcting the grammar. You want your child to see his or her own voice, not yours. As your child becomes more comfortable with reading, you can suggest grammar corrections. If possible, type your child's words in a font similar to what appears in his or her books. Print your child's writing and help him or her add illustrations. Create a binder containing your child's stories and ideas. Use this binder as your go-to when your child is not interested in reading other material.

If your child is assigned a book for which a movie has been made, see the movie first. Once a child has seen the movie, he or she may be motivated to read the book because he or she will have a context for the reading and understand it better.

As your child becomes a proficient silent reader, he or she may want to stop reading aloud with you. You should be sensitive to this change and limit the amount of oral reading you do together. Instead, you can each read your own books at the same time.

How to Provide Reading Instruction to a Child with Dyslexia

In addition to reading with your child daily, you can also provide formal reading instruction a few times a week. The key to successfully working with your child is to stop *before* he or she becomes upset. Spending too much time on a skill that your child cannot yet master can reinforce his or her negative thoughts about reading. Some of the instructional practices that follow can be done during your reading-together time, but others are best done in short one- to five-minute sessions a few times a week.

Recognizing That Printed Words Have Meaning

Help your child recognize that printed words have the same meaning as spoken words. If you were to read a sentence like "Tom swung the stick," swing your arm as you say the word "swung." Throw your body into it. Even the most mundane material can be read with emotion to convey meaning.

Point out the way printed words correspond to images and actions. If you read the sentence "Ann sprang up!" and there is an illustration of Ann springing up, point it out so your child can connect the word "sprang" with an action. I do this all the time when working with children who are just beginning to read. It makes reading fun.

Recognizing Letters and Short Words

Children with dyslexia frequently struggle to remember the alphabet. One of the difficulties they may have is that they confuse letters (d/b, p/q, n/m, w/v, f/t). To a skilled reader, the differences between letters are easy to detect. Children with dyslexia often cannot make these distinctions. Additionally, the alphabet is frequently learned through song. Children with dyslexia, however, may be unable to remember the rhythmic nature of the ABC song. A further complication is that children with dyslexia have difficulty with sequential memory as a whole (letters of the alphabet, months of the year, days of the week). Because learning the alphabet is essential for school success, make practicing the alphabet a regular part of your literacy activities. Find a place to display the alphabet in your home so that it is easy to practice often.

In a light-hearted manner, see if your child can begin to recognize some letters or short words on a page. A good place to start is by asking your child to find the first letter in his or her name and point it out. For example, if your child's name begins with a "C" and you come across the word "cup," point out the connection. Next time you come to a word that starts with a "C," say, "Whose name starts with a 'C?'" Write a big "C" on a piece of paper. In time, do the same with other familiar names like Mom, Dad, and Grandpa. Build on this skill by using creative approaches, such as using Scrabble tiles or letters printed on cards to show your child how other small words are spelled. Keep your child interested by adding in his or her favorite foods, colors, and animals.

You can deepen your child's connection to letters and small words by having him or her write them out. Write a normal-size letter and have your child say the sound the letter makes as he or she writes a very large version of the letter on a big sheet of paper or a whiteboard. This strategy works around the difficulty many children with dyslexia have with fine motor skills. Children are also more likely to draw a letter or word if it feels like a fun activity rather than an academic lesson. You can also have your child sculpt the letter out of clay or trace the letter with his or her finger in sand, shaving cream, or whipped cream.

Understanding Phonics

Reading difficulties frequently emerge at the beginning: recognizing letters, the sounds that letters make, and the sounds that combinations of letters (th, ch, sh) make. If a child has trouble recognizing any of these patterns, a domino effect can occur. Down the road, the child might have ongoing difficulty with reading and reading comprehension.

According to reading expert Sally Shaywitz, phonemic awareness develops when children learn letters and their sounds, and then learn to build and change words by "pulling them apart, pushing them together and moving letters within a word" (2005). The more familiar term "phonics" encompasses phonemic awareness and the ability to sound out words from left to right, identify rhymes, recognize syllables, and recognize words within a sentence.

Phonics is an approach to teaching reading that emphasizes the sounds that letters and letter combinations make. Phonics prioritizes sounding words out as a means of learning to read and also as a way to accurately read new or unfamiliar words. Phonics has long been the favored approach to reading instruction, especially for children with dyslexia.

There are a number of different ways you can begin to incorporate phonics instruction into your work with your child. For example, point out that certain letters make certain sounds. Have fun with letters such as "p" and the *puh* sound it makes. Point out common consonant combination sounds (for example, *ch, sh, gl, pl, nd, ng*) and how they sound in the words you are reading to your child. Perhaps your child's name begins with "Ch" or "Gl." This is a great opportunity to help your child see the connection. This will strengthen his or her recognition of the sound this letter combination makes the next time he or she runs across a word that begins with "Ch" or "Gl." Introduce short vowel sounds (for example, *ah, eh, ih, uh*) and then long vowel sounds (for example, *ay, ee, eye, oh, oo*). After that, introduce vowel combination sounds (for example, ea [*ee* or *ay*], ou [*oo* or *ow*]). As your child becomes more skilled, begin to introduce more complex letter combinations and their sounds.

Recognizing Syllables and Compound Words

It's essential for all children, especially those with dyslexia, to learn how to break larger words into smaller units. We need to give these children every tool possible to decode words so they will be less likely to skip over them while reading. When a child looks at the word "education," he or she needs to be able to recognize the syllables in order to sound the word out. As a parent, you can rewrite the word spread out into syllables (ed/u/ca/tion). Point out how each syllable has its own sound, and then string the sounds together. Many children learn syllables through the technique of clapping at each sound. But for children whose language-based learning difficulties impact their auditory processing, visual aids are often better.

Many children with dyslexia are particularly good at pattern recognition. Point out to your child the patterns for sight words like "could," "would," and "should." Your child will also need explicit instruction to learn that "tion" = *shun* and that "ch" makes the hard *ka* sound in the words "school," "ache," "anchor," and "architect."

As you help your child break larger words into smaller parts, you can also teach him or her compound words. Words like "cupcake," "weekend," and "basketball" can be broken into individual words. For example, point out that "cupcake" is composed of "cup" and "cake." Then draw pictures of a cup and a cake to help illustrate the compound nature of the word.

Teaching Common Sight and High-Frequency Words

One of the most important objectives in any type of reading instruction is to help a child see and automatically know a word. For example, if the child sees a word with the letters "t," "h," and "e," and spends any amount of time trying to sound it out, his or her reading has been impacted. But if a child can see these letters and immediately recognize them as "the," he or she will be able to continue reading efficiently.

Automaticity is the ability to recognize words in print automatically. We know a child has achieved true automaticity when he or she rapidly identifies words not only in isolation but also in context. If you feel your child has the bandwidth, help him or her begin to recognize common sight and high-frequency words. Many of these words can only be learned by sight because they do not follow a phonetic pattern (e.g., could, are).

High-frequency words include "the," "of," "is," "you," "use," and "who." You can find lists of both high-frequency and sight words on the Internet.

With your child, create a list of high-frequency words he or she might already know (for example, "a," "at," "I," "in," "is," "it," "if," "up"). Point out to your child that these are very common words. Keep a running list of the words your child is learning to read. This will keep him or her motivated to learn more words. There are around one hundred words that make up almost half of all the words your child is likely to encounter while reading in elementary school. If your child can master those 100 words, he or she can already read many of the words he or she will encounter!

Here is a drill I have used for years with many different types of learners to teach common sight and high-frequency words. It always works well. For a downloadable version, visit this book's website: http://www.newharbinger.com/40989.

An Easy Way to Learn Sight Words

The goal of these steps is to make sure your child is always able to correctly recognize and pronounce the words you are working on.

1. Write common sight words on individual index cards. Neatly print the letters. The idea is to imitate how the words will appear in printed text. Cards written in cursive are not as effective in helping your child recognize the targeted word when encountered later in a book.

2. Place no more than ten cards face up. If you are starting with unfamiliar words, use no more than five at a time. Use only the amount of words that your child can engage with in a meaningful way.

3. Let your child study the words on the cards until he or she is ready to read one.

4. If your child says the word correctly, put it to the side. If your child mispronounces the word, tell him or her the correct pronunciation and put the card into a different pile.

5. Complete the process until you have two piles of cards: the cards your child read correctly the first time and the cards your child missed, which will be used in the second round.

6. Place the cards for round two on the table face up.

7. Ask your child to look at the words for as long as he or she needs to in order to see if he or she can recognize any of them given more time. You can say, "Once you are pretty sure you know a word, point to the card and say the word."

8. If your child reads the word correctly, put the card to the side.

9. If he or she mispronounces the word again, say, "That's close." Show your child the difference by writing the word he or she said directly underneath the word on the card. Point out how the words are similar and how they are different. If your child mispronounces the word "cookie" by saying "kooky," tell him or her that what he or she said made sense. Then help him or her differentiate between the words.

10. When you do this drill in the future, your child can read both words written on the card.

11. If your child does not feel comfortable choosing a card, say the word aloud and ask your child to locate it.

Understanding Punctuation

You can begin to teach your child to recognize punctuation by pointing out how it is used. Take a passage, no matter how simple, and circle, highlight, or underline the punctuation marks. Ask your child to point to the different punctuation marks you've noted and discuss what each mark means and how it affects the sentence. Practice reading the passage emphasizing appropriate intonation and punctuation. Use a wide assortment of reading material, including plays, comic strips, and short stories.

Scarborough's Reading Rope

Reading expert Hollis Scarborough created this wonderful illustration. I find it useful when explaining to parents and teachers the wide array of capacities required to be a skilled reader. You may find it useful too when considering the many different skills you are helping your child develop.

THE MANY STRANDS THAT ARE WOVEN INTO SKILLED READING

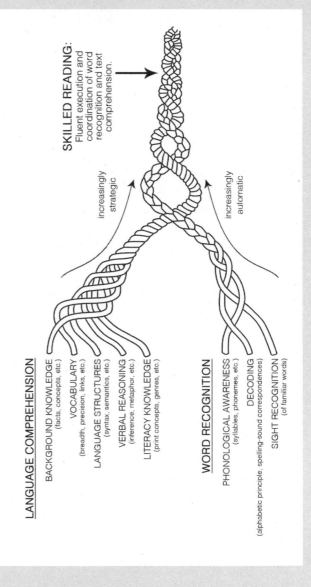

LANGUAGE COMPREHENSION

BACKGROUND KNOWLEDGE
(facts, concepts, etc.)

VOCABULARY
(breadth, precision, links, etc.)

LANGUAGE STRUCTURES
(syntax, semantics, etc.)

VERBAL REASONING
(inference, metaphor, etc.)

LITERACY KNOWLEDGE
(print concepts, genres, etc.)

WORD RECOGNITION

PHONOLOGICAL AWARENESS
(syllables, phonemes, etc.)

DECODING
(alphabetic principle, spelling-sound correspondences)

SIGHT RECOGNITION
(of familiar words)

increasingly strategic

increasingly automatic

SKILLED READING:
Fluent execution and coordination of word recognition and text comprehension.

How to Develop Your Child's Vocabulary

Well-developed vocabulary is critical for good listening and reading comprehension. Many children with language-based learning difficulties struggle to learn new words, which puts them at a significant disadvantage relative to their peers when trying to manage the demands of school, social interactions, and self-expression. Learning new words requires that an individual recognize the word and connect it to an idea or meaning. Many children with LBLDs are unable to connect meaning to words even if they are familiar with the words.

In a surprising twist, some children with language-based learning difficulties have an outstanding ability to learn new words. For these children, vocabulary development offers many benefits: it's rewarding, it promotes a positive mindset about their ability to be successful learners, and it allows children to draw on this strength when facing reading and listening comprehension challenges.

Children with LBLDs do not need to be highly skilled at reading to become skilled at vocabulary. Significant vocabulary development can be accomplished through speaking. Moreover, teaching vocabulary is easy, fun, and productive, as long as you follow these key principles:

- Show your enthusiasm for language. From time to time, use an unusual word or a word that might be a little above your child's age range. See if it piques his or her interest.

- Stay away from words with meanings that have no relevance to your child or you. For example, "erinaceous"—no offense to hedgehogs or things that are hedgehog-like!

- Provide definitions. If you want to help your child learn how to find definitions, great! Just don't combine dictionary or research skills with vocabulary development. Provide the definition as many times as your child requests it. Never make your child self-conscious about not remembering the meaning of a word.

- Avoid directly quizzing your child on the meaning of a word. Instead, use the word frequently and in as many different contexts as you reasonably can.

- Don't ask your child to spell the word you are teaching unless he or she loves to spell and write—in which case, go for it!

- Emphasize breadth over depth. It is much better to have a fairly good understanding of a lot of different words than a deep understanding of only a few words. When teaching vocabulary to your child, arrive at the simplest definition. A synonym is often the best place to start. There is room, however, to occasionally go down a rabbit hole with a word. Find a word your child really likes and help him or her do some research on the word. Help your child become an "expert" on the word, learning its origin and how its meaning and even spelling may have changed over time. Create a poster to display words that are part of your child's "collection."

- You can use the drill described in "An Easy Way to Learn Sight Words" to teach vocabulary. Simply use both sides of the index cards. Write vocabulary words on one side and their synonyms on the back.

How to Teach Advanced Reading Skills

As with many things we teach children, we are not going to be effective trying to teach everything at once. This is especially true of reading skills. As your child becomes more skilled at reading, you can begin to work on additional foundational skills such as accuracy, fluency, and reading rate to improve reading comprehension. Remember that you are trying to conserve your child's energy to learn the content, so being as supportive as possible as you practice the strategies that follow is absolutely key. Additional advice can be found on the handy, downloadable checklist, Tips for Teaching Advanced Reading Skills, provided on this book's website: http://www.newharbinger.com/40989.

Accuracy

Reading accuracy means correctly reading every word on a page and demonstrating an appropriate interpretation of punctuation. Children with dyslexia need plenty of opportunities to master this skill. Becoming a more accurate reader will help your child overcome the tendency to skip words and punctuation while reading. To help, you can teach your child ways to decode difficult or new words.

When you work on reading accuracy, select content that your child likes and that is one to two years *above* his or her reading level (not grade level). Then take turns reading.

Pay careful attention to reading errors. When your child comes to a new or unfamiliar word, give him or her a fair amount of time to try to sound it out. If your child would like your help, you can write the word in syllables and isolate complex phonetic patterns. You want your child to work on sounding out the word. If there is an error your child always makes with a simple word he or she has already learned, bring it to his or her attention. Discuss some reasons he or she may be making this error. Finally, you can incorporate the misread words and new vocabulary (except highly unusual words, unusual proper nouns, and words that are way beyond your child's reading level) into the drill "An Easy Way to Learn Sight Words."

Fluency

Reading fluency is the smooth reading of material with a reasonably high degree of accuracy and observation of punctuation. To promote reading fluency in your child, begin by selecting any high-interest reading material one to two years *below* your child's reading level (not grade level). Then trade off reading page for page, paragraph for paragraph, or even sentence for sentence, if necessary. Model appropriate intonation and observation of punctuation.

When it's your child's turn to read, only correct your child if he or she asks for help. If your child does ask for help with a word, simply provide the help and allow him or her to continue reading. You want to make this reading exercise as unencumbered as possible.

If, however, the error your child makes completely alters the meaning of what he or she is reading, correct him or her. Likewise, if there is an error your child repeatedly makes, bring it to his or her attention.

As with all reading activities, record new and misread words onto index cards and complete the "Easy Way to Learn Sight Words" drill. Remember that you do not need to record highly unusual words, unusual proper nouns, and words that are way beyond your child's reading level.

Rate

It's important to help your child increase his or her reading rate. Because your child must maintain focus in order to read quickly, reading rate exercises often result in a higher level of engagement with the text. To help improve your child's reading rate, do speed drills with sight words. Have your child read words from the sight word index cards as quickly as he or she can. Once your child is comfortable with single words, start using phrase cards, whereby you have two-, three-, or four-word phrases on index cards. Phrase cards are easy to download from numerous sites on the Internet. Phrase cards should not contain new or unfamiliar words.

Hold your hand over a familiar phrase. Ask your child, "Are you ready?" Then remove your hand for a second, showing your child the phrase. Cover it again quickly and ask your child to recite the phrase. In time, have your child read a sentence from a book. Then have him or her read it again, faster. Then have your child read it a third time, even faster still. Eventually, you can do the same with short paragraphs. Most children enjoy speeding things up, but don't force your child beyond what is fun for him or her. Having fun is the most important thing. Speed drills in short bursts are the way to go.

Comprehension

As we saw in Hollis Scarborough's Reading Rope illustration earlier in this chapter, skilled reading is the culmination of many different skills. Therefore, helping your child improve reading accuracy, fluency, and rate is key. Reading comprehension can also be enhanced as follows: Select material at your child's reading level (not grade level). Have your child read a page or two aloud. Reading aloud will allow you to monitor for any problems your child might have with the material. Start by asking very general questions such as, "What was that about?" As your child becomes more skilled at reading, begin to ask more detailed questions. Once your child becomes a skilled reader, have him or her read sections silently and then follow the same process by first asking general questions and later more detailed questions about the material.

If your child makes a lot of errors while reading or does not seem to understand what a reading passage is about, read aloud to your child and help him or her understand the material. Or you can find texts that present the same material in simpler terms. For example, if your child is in a high school biology class learning about photosynthesis, you might find that the topic is more clearly explained in a child's science book, which likely has better illustrations, larger print, and clearer definitions. While reading literature, online summaries provided by study-support resources such as Sparknotes (http://www.sparknotes.com) and Shmoop (https://www.shmoop.com) can be a major help. There are an increasing number of excellent short videos on Youtube that provide summaries of the major works of literature. These videos are a terrific starting point for a big reading assignment.

As your child gets older and becomes a more skilled reader, introduce strategies such as previewing chapters; reading chapter titles, headings, subheadings, and key terms; and reviewing illustrations, diagrams, and graphs. These steps help your child anticipate what the text will cover. Before beginning reading, help your child think about what the purpose of the selection is. Think about what your child's teacher might want the students to understand and remember.

While reading, encourage your child to periodically reflect on what he or she is reading and learning. These short pauses have the added benefit of allowing your child to consolidate information as it is being poured into his or her brain.

Finally, summarize the material together. Help your child develop the capacity to jot down a few notes about what he or she has just read. Or have your child highlight important words or sentences that you point out (otherwise, your child may highlight the entire page!). Either way, these tasks can be exceedingly difficult for a child with dyslexia. It is essential you become highly involved in the steps needed for accurate reading comprehension.

How to Manage the Reading Demands of Homework

Parents frequently ask me how they can best support their children with the reading demands of school. In an effort to give them a framework, I have created a hierarchy of reading support (which is also available for download at the website for this book: http://www.newharbinger .com/40989). It consists of four levels, organized from the least support needed to the most. Based on your child's individual needs, you can select which level of support to provide. Because the priority is learning content and completing the assignment, I always advise erring on the side of higher levels of support.

Levels of Reading Support

Level 1: Your child reads silently on his or her own.

Read the material yourself so that you can determine how much your child comprehends.

Before your child begins reading, activate his or her mind by asking him or her to think about what information is supposed to be gained by reading.

When your child is finished reading, check for understanding by having your child explain to you what has been read, clarify misunderstandings, fill in gaps, and provide opportunities to reinforce what is being learned.

Engage in a discussion about what was read.

Ask your child to create a list of key ideas and words gleaned from the reading.

Use illustrations and diagrams to help your child better understand the material.

Level 2: Your child reads aloud to you.

Before your child begins reading to you, activate his or her mind by asking him or her to think about what information is supposed to be gained by reading.

As your child reads, check for understanding by having your child explain to you what has been read, clarify misunderstandings, fill in gaps, and provide opportunities to reinforce what is being learned.

Engage in a discussion about what was read.

With your child, create a list of key ideas and words gleaned from the reading.

Use illustrations and diagrams to help your child better understand the material.

Level 3: You read aloud to your child.

Before you begin reading to your child, activate his or her mind by asking him or her to think about what information is supposed to be gained by reading.

As you read, check for understanding by having your child explain to you what has been read, clarify misunderstandings, fill in gaps, and provide opportunities to reinforce what is being learned.

Use tone to emphasize key concepts or plot points.

Engage in a discussion about what was read.

With your child, create a list of key ideas and words gleaned from the reading.

Use illustrations and diagrams to help your child better understand the material.

Level 4: You read and summarize for your child.

This approach is especially helpful when there is a large amount of reading assigned.

The point is that your child needs to learn the content. There is nothing wrong with approaching reading support in this way. *Forcing children to read before they are able to learn from reading is counterproductive.*

Engage in a discussion about what you read.

With your child, create a list of key ideas and words gleaned from the reading.

Use illustrations and diagrams to help your child better understand the material.

Teaching How to Follow Written Directions

It's also important for a slowly emerging reader to understand and follow complicated written directions. You should facilitate as much as needed in order to help your child develop direction-reading and -following skills.

When you sit down together to do homework, begin by saying, "Let's look at the directions. Would you like to read them, or should I?" Once the directions are read, ask, "What do we need to do here?" If your child doesn't know, say, "Let's read them again." If you sense that your child will become frustrated by reading the directions a second time, don't make him or her read them again. It's important that your child remain emotionally regulated. Instead, you can say, "What I think they want us to do is _____." Next, show your child how you arrived at that conclusion.

Bypass Strategies for Reading Assignments and Chapter Review Questions

You can find additional tips on how to support your child by visiting this book's website: http://www.newharbinger.com/40989. There you'll find numerous ways to work around your child's slowly emerging reading skills so that he or she can ultimately learn what is expected.

Conclusion

Helping your child with the reading demands of homework is an excellent way to ensure your child's success now and in the future. There may be times when your child needs to learn concepts, times when he or she needs to get the work done, and times when he or she needs practice reading and answering questions. What's crucial is that you stay focused on the learning objective, even if this means supporting your child by bypassing the skills that are slow to emerge in your son or daughter.

When you support your child with tasks that are beyond his or her skills, you set up your child to succeed in school.

When you help your child complete homework, you circumvent the challenges that arise from his or her slowly emerging reading capacities. The quality of life in your home will be better, and your child will eventually improve at school because you will have made it easier for him or her to learn and remember the content being taught. Expediting homework will also create the time you need to read together daily to help improve your child's reading skills.

CHAPTER 7

Dysgraphia: Unable to Write in a Writing World

As difficult as it is for a child with dyslexia to become a proficient reader, writing can be an even more difficult skill to master. Writing requires many of the same skills needed to be a proficient reader *plus* many additional ones. Children are expected to master the physical aspects of writing, such as letter formation and spacing, along with spelling, punctuation, grammar, syntax, and other areas of writing mechanics.

Good writing also requires a broad set of executive functioning skills, including organization, focus, attention to detail, and sustained effort. Children with LBLDs are often delayed in these areas. As with reading disabilities, we can minimize the impact of a child's writing disability with early identification and intervention. No matter how old your child is, if you recognize that he or she is struggling with writing, you should intervene as soon as possible.

Much as a struggling reader cannot be expected to learn content from written text, a struggling writer cannot be expected to demonstrate knowledge through independent writing. Therefore, I recommend working with your child in a highly collaborative way. This approach ensures that writing assignments are completed and your child becomes a skilled writer.

In this chapter, you'll learn how to create a culture of writing in your home, how to develop your child's foundational writing skills, and how to write collaboratively with your child.

Creating a Culture of Writing in Your Home

Writing can be an engaging activity for all children. Just as we encourage kids to run around and chase a ball before forcing them to adhere to the rules of soccer, we should make the process of learning to write fun, and worry about grammar a little later.

In the previous chapter, we discussed how creating a culture of spoken language in your home promotes reading skill development in your child. In this spirit, strive to create a culture of writing at home. Writing can be an extracurricular activity in your home much in the way I encourage reading to be. As with reading, the more a child practices writing, the better a writer he or she will become, no matter his or her age.

The strategies in this chapter will help you approach writing with your child in a fun way. What you write is entirely up to you and your child. Your child can choose to record the day's activities, create a series of short stories, review a video, or journal personal musings. Whenever you write collaboratively with your child, whether it is for a school assignment or during your extracurricular writing, you'll need to adjust your support to match your child's needs, which will change from year to year, week to week, and even day to day. But on average, try making writing activities something you do two or three times a week.

Encouraging a Reluctant Writer

I would like to offer a cautionary note here: When you write collaboratively with your child, whether it is for schoolwork or homegrown writing activities, don't force your child to write beyond his or her capacities. For many struggling writers, their first draft is their final draft. We want writing to have a playlike quality so that your child will write more often without worrying about grammar. In time, your child will acquire the skills needed to improve punctuation and sentence structure.

Encourage speaking. You can begin developing your child's writing skills at any age, even well before he or she can form letters, by encouraging speaking. Ask your child questions about things that interest him or her. Help your child elaborate on what he or she is saying by asking: "How? Why? What happened next?" Contribute ideas and information that will help your child learn how to expand on what he or she expresses. Finally, encourage storytelling. Your child can become a terrific storyteller long before he or she acquires the skills to write.

Encourage drawing. All children are natural artists, and luckily, drawing is another precursor to writing. Drawing promotes creative thinking, thought organization, planning, problem solving, fine motor skills, and concentration—all of which are related to writing. On a regular basis, help your young child learn to draw basic shapes such as circles, squares, and triangles. Scribbling is great too! Encourage your child to create representations for things like trees, houses, people, and animals. Go easy on formal drawing instruction and the expectation that your child's drawing will look like yours. Nothing makes a child more self-conscious than having his or her artistic efforts compared to those of an adult. Even as your child gets older, continue to encourage drawing; teens and young adults benefit from drawing on a regular basis too.

Create a calm space to write. To set the stage for writing together, dedicate an area in your home for a "writer's workshop." The area should be well lit and comfortable. Ask your child what seating arrangement he or she would like. Some children prefer to be in very close proximity to their parent, while others prefer to have a little distance.

Start a library. Even if your writing sessions only involve writing one sentence at a time, you will have a fairly complete piece of work within a few weeks that can be stored in a binder—the beginnings of a library. Your child can add illustrations later, or you might consider starting with the illustrations, and then add the written component later. Either way, you will build a body of writing that your child can choose to read from when you read together.

Allow your child to dictate his or her thoughts. You want your child to focus on developing ideas without being slowed down by the process of writing. Bypass your child's slowly emerging writing and/or keyboarding skills by becoming a scribe: write or type your child's thoughts as he or she says them. Go easy on correcting the grammar. You want your child to appreciate his or her own voice, not yours. You can help your child refine and clarify his or her thoughts later. We want children with dysgraphia to know they have good ideas that can be captured in writing and that they can use the process of writing to develop and organize those ideas.

Try engaging and fun activities. When children struggle with writing, they need extra support to make writing exercises engaging. There are a variety of ways you can make writing fun: Ask your child to make a drawing or cut out an interesting photograph from a magazine. Then ask him or her to dictate a story about the drawing or photograph. You can also ask your child to dictate a letter to a family member, a character in his or her favorite book, or even your pet. Another activity is to have your child dictate his or her autobiography or the biography of a family member. Create a collection of your child's writing, and frequently read selections to him or her. This will motivate your child to write more.

Work on developing ideas. Teaching your child how to develop a narrative is best done by engaging him or her in a conversation. Ask your child questions that keep his or her storyline going. Along the way, encourage your child to use transition words like "first," "then," "next," and "finally." Encourage your child to ask him or herself how, why, what if, and what then. Model your own thought process by explaining to your child how you arrived at a question or conclusion.

Go easy on the mechanics. When you are helping your child with a writing assignment, refrain from focusing heavily on correcting his or her work. But when your child seems ready, experiment with various sentence types and structures. Try writing one long run-on sentence and then help your child break it up into shorter sentences. You can also help your child explore different words to express his or her ideas by using a thesaurus. When it comes to the correct spelling of a word, be okay with whatever takes the least amount of effort—even if that means you provide the right spelling. Having a child look up a word will slow down the process, make it less fun, and diminish motivation.

How to Develop Foundational Writing Skills

Once the basic capacities for writing have emerged, you can begin to explore foundational writing skills. I always remind parents not to underestimate the value of helping their children learn to write by hand, even though computers are helpful for all children, especially those with LBLDs. The slow, deliberate process of writing by hand reinforces letter recognition, spelling, word choice, and punctuation. Furthermore, writing by hand is a critical skill that your child will always need. Even under the best circumstances, there will be times when writing by hand is necessary, so it is important that all children acquire some degree of handwriting competency.

Keyboarding, however, offers an excellent bypass strategy for children who find writing by hand difficult. Keyboarding provides your child with an easy way to spell words, write sentences, and generate stories. Well-developed keyboarding skills are essential in order for your child to navigate most of the writing assignments he or she will have for years to come. As a parent, you will need to balance instruction in both handwriting and keyboarding so that your child is able to benefit from what each method has to offer.

Letter Recognition

Letter recognition is very challenging for children with LBLDs. Make sure your home has a place where the alphabet is in plain view with print (not cursive) lowercase and uppercase letters. Add an image that corresponds to the letter (for example, an apple with "A," a banana with "B," and so on). Creating an illustrated alphabet together will help reinforce letter recognition and letter sounds. Review the alphabet frequently with your child.

If you are helping your child learn how to form letters, work on a letter or two at a time. I like to start with A, B, C, and then choose other letters, often the first letter of the child's name.

You may need to spend extra time working on certain letters. Most children with LBLDs need additional help learning how to distinguish between visually similar letters like d/b, g/q, m/n, and so on. One way to do this is to copy a page from a book and have your child circle all the b's but ignore all the d's.

When you feel that your child is ready for a bigger challenge, have him or her write short words. As your child's skills improve, he or she can begin writing short sentences. First, write down in clear print a sentence your child says. Then provide your child with a piece of lined paper and have him or her copy the sentence. Sometimes it is helpful to put short lines where each word is supposed to go. If the sentence has four words, I will provide four short lines as a guide. For example: _____. You might need to point to each word as your child writes it. In some cases, I will actually write the words very lightly and have my student trace over my writing. The key is to provide the amount of scaffolding your child needs to stay engaged in the writing activity.

Spelling

You can help your child with spelling by encouraging an appreciation of how many words he or she already knows how to spell. The idea is to make sure your child is 100 percent successful. Success breeds success, so it's important to design all instruction for a child with language-based learning difficulties around opportunities for success.

Start with words like "a," "I," "in," "is," "it," "on," "as," "at," "an," "if," "be," and "up." Not only are these easy words to spell, but they also are among the most commonly used. Next, try your child's name. Children are highly motivated to spell their own names and the names of those important to them, like Mom, Dad, siblings, relatives, and pets.

To practice a spelling word, write the word on a piece of paper and have your child trace over it a few times. Once your child is ready, have him or her write it on a fresh piece of paper. Allow your child to look at your original spelling. This visual check reinforces your child's capacity to hold information in his or her working memory. Next, write a simple sentence. If the spelling word is your child's name, write "My name is _____." Have your child fill in the blank with his or her name.

Ask your child what words he or she would like to learn how to spell. Giving your child a choice will help motivate him or her and reduce anxiety. Once your child has chosen a word he or she wants to learn how to spell, write down the word. Let your child practice writing the word as many times as he or she wants. Then ask your child if he or she is ready to try to spell the word. When ready, leave the word on the table but give your child a fresh sheet of paper. Allow your child to write the word.

To prepare for spelling tests, have your child practice writing the words as many times as he or she needs to feel comfortable. When your child is ready for a practice test, provide him or her with a blank sheet of paper. Say the word and have your child write it down. Check his or her spelling. If the word is spelled correctly, move on. If not, show your child the correct spelling of the word and ask him or her to write the word correctly three times. After this, move on to the next word on the list. When you reach the end of the list, turn the page over and repeat the misspelled word(s). Do not move on to the next word until your child has written the word correctly three times.

When you work on spelling, pay attention to any phonetic patterns that are challenging for your child, like "ight" in "night" or the "tch" in "pitch." Practice spelling similar words using the approach described above.

Talk with your child about common spelling rules. Children with dysgraphia benefit from engaging in thinking about spelling. There are a number of resources that will teach you both about common spelling rules, such as doubling a consonant when adding "ing" (running) or when to use "ch" versus "tch" (bunch vs. batch).

Capitalization and Punctuation

To help your child recognize that the first letter of every sentence is capitalized, photocopy a page or two from your child's favorite book.

Have your child circle the first letter of each sentence. This activity will draw your child's attention to this important detail. In time, you can repeat the process to illustrate the capitalization of proper nouns.

To reinforce your child's command of basic punctuation, make sure he or she understands the three basic forms of end punctuation: period, question mark, and exclamation point. Invent or print out sentences with the end punctuation missing. Ask your child to determine what the correct end punctuation should be. Allow your child to ask you questions, and, if needed, read the sentences aloud to your child.

Like the exercise for recognizing capital letters, you can print a page or two from your child's favorite book and ask him or her to circle the end punctuation of each sentence. Once your child has mastered end punctuation, you can begin to work on other forms of punctuation, like apostrophes and quotation marks.

How to Collaborate on Writing Assignments

Writing for school may not always be fun, but by approaching writing in a highly collaborative way, you will help your child develop his or her ideas and produce finished work as efficiently as possible. This efficiency will make it less likely that your child will resist completing homework. If your child has dysgraphia, writing assignments may need to be supported through high school and into college. Professional writers enjoy the support of collaborators, editors, and proofreaders; there is no reason to deny similar support to your child.

Before we delve into the specific ways you can partner with your child in writing, let's look at some general grade-level standards and how to help your child meet them.

Elementary School Writing Assignments

By the end of elementary school, children should be able to write short essays that are logically structured and grammatically correct. Review with your child that a complete sentence is a complete thought, starts with a capital letter, and ends with a punctuation mark. Stories and essays have a beginning, middle, and end. Discuss some of your child's favorite stories and point out the beginning, middle, and end. These discussions will help your child understand the need for structure in his or her own writing.

Once your child understands general structure, delve into paragraph structure. Explain why each paragraph should begin with a topic sentence that introduces the paragraph's main idea. Help your child carefully draft a topic sentence and then provide him or her with guidance to generate supporting sentences. Help your child learn how to stay on topic throughout a given paragraph. Each line in the paragraph should relate back to the topic sentence.

Once your child understands paragraph structure, help him or her write several paragraphs on one topic and then make sure each paragraph transitions to the next. If the flow isn't working, help your child see how shifting the order of paragraphs or sentences within paragraphs can often make writing more logical.

Continue to function as your child's scribe. When your child isn't able to generate ideas right away, help by providing prompts and transcribing what he or she says. For example, if your child is assigned a paper about trees, you might say, "What are some benefits of planting trees?" You can also prompt your child by reminding him or her of things he or she has said in the past about the topic: "Remember when we were at the park and you pointed out how the trees provided a nice place for birds and squirrels to live? What if I wrote that down for you as a starting point for your paper?" Build on this process to generate as many sentences as you can.

If you find that your child is straying too far from the topic, bring him or her back by saying things like, "A few minutes ago, you were speaking about how the trees in the park provided a nice place for birds and squirrels to live. What are some other thoughts you have on that topic?"

If you find that your child is running out of energy for the writing task, review a few of the interesting things he or she has said and see if any of them spark a couple more thoughts. As your child's energy runs down, agree on a finishing time and hold to it.

Middle and High School Writing Assignments

As your child gets older, he or she will be expected to write independently. Even though your child is older, it does not mean help is not needed to make sure all of his or her ideas have been clearly written. Writing assignments in middle and high school become more complex, and your child will benefit from your collaboration. This is especially true for research papers, feared by many a student—and perhaps just as many a parent! Over the years, I've seen wonderful students virtually paralyzed by such assignments.

• *Kaia's (and My!) Story*

Some years ago, I worked with Kaia, a bright and motivated eleventh-grader with significant dysgraphia. Kaia had enrolled in a particularly challenging history class and was assigned a research paper. As I reviewed the paper's guidelines, I was reminded of an experience I had had myself, many years earlier in high school.

Halfway through my eleventh-grade year, despite my significant struggles in school due largely to dyslexia, I decided to sign up for a challenging research-writing course. The teacher, Mrs. Longo, knew me well and suggested I reconsider taking her class, but I assured her that I was up for the challenge.

There is an important lesson here. Teenagers benefit from being trusted to decide what challenges they want to take on. Had I been forbidden to take this class, it would have further lowered my self-esteem. If your child wants to take a challenging class, you should encourage him or her to do so. He or she will be surrounded by motivated, ambitious students. My class kept me feeling like a college-bound student even when the odds were against me.

Kaia's (and My!) Story (continued)

For the first couple of weeks, things went quite well. The class discussed the important world events we might choose as topics. I excelled in conversation, so I thought I was home free! But then we were expected to create an outline over the weekend. All weekend, I thought about the assignment. I knew what the finished product was supposed to be, but I couldn't figure out how to produce it. On Sunday night, I was consumed by overwhelming anxiety about what Monday would bring.

When Monday came, I had nothing to turn in, nor did I have anything to turn in on the many days that followed. Virtually every day, Mrs. Longo would gently remind me that if I didn't do the work, I would fail her class. I would nod my head and smile. I assured her that I would do the required work. But deep down inside, I knew I was going to fail—but not because I wanted to. Left to my own devices, I simply did not have the ability, or the tools, to manage all of the logistics that go into crafting a research paper.

When I worked with Kaia, I provided the support I wished someone had offered me. I systematically broke down each step into parts she could understand and contribute to. I actively engaged her in the project through conversation by acting as her scribe and by making sure we adhered to a reasonable timetable. I know this approach is time consuming, but if your child has dysgraphia, this type of support is needed.

How to Write with Your Child

Think of yourself as a project manager when you write with your child. You will need to stay apprised of all writing assignments. For each assignment, you will need to familiarize yourself with the directions so that you and your child are not surprised by a specific requirement, like interviewing a local expert or building a model. Break down assignments into smaller pieces to complete the paper on time. Then sit with your child and work together to complete each piece as efficiently as possible. This will teach your child how to complete assignments step by step. For a handy downloadable checklist of the tips that follow, visit this book's website: http://www.newharbinger.com/40989.

Choosing a Topic and Starting Research

Discuss the writing assignment with your child. Make sure your child is aware of the specific requirements. Help your child choose a topic that interests him or her. If the topic is assigned and your child isn't showing enthusiasm for it, promote his or her interest by exploring the topic on the Internet or checking out books from the library. Devote time to watching informative videos or high-interest movies related to the subject of the research paper. Visit a local museum or business that has some relationship to the topic. By organically introducing your child to the subject of his or her research paper, he or she will begin to feel like an expert on the topic before you begin the writing process. This will promote his or her motivation to work on the research paper and apply a higher level of effort to it.

Help your child identify relevant information in the various sources you have gathered. This aspect of writing is often one of the most difficult for children with LBLDs because it demands well-developed reading skills and the capacity to strategically locate and record important information. As a parent of a child with dysgraphia, you will need to provide a high level of support by reading material aloud to your child and helping him or her recognize when something is worth using in the paper.

When working with middle and high school students, I find that elementary-level books make the process of reading about the topic as easy as possible. Books of this type can be found in the children's section of a library. Read and review a few of these books with your child. Then help him or her develop an organization system for all of the materials that you have gathered. Help your child neatly compile the research.

Starting to Write

Begin the writing process by asking your child what he or she knows about the topic. Write down everything your child says, even if some thoughts don't seem relevant. You want your child to know that you value what he or she is saying. This will prompt your child to contribute even more ideas.

As your child dictates to you, provide prompts and suggestions. Encourage your child to elaborate where necessary to clarify ideas. Offer suggestions and help your child fill in gaps that might exist in the writing.

Sometimes it can be helpful to create an outline before the writing process begins. Other times, it makes more sense to start the writing process and then create an outline later based on the written material your child generates with your help. I have seen many instances where the outline gets in the way of the natural flow and development of ideas. You should do whichever works best for your child and you.

Encourage your child to think about the audience. For most school assignments, the audience will be your child's teacher, and each teacher has his or her own preferences and expectations. If the assignment is intended for a specific audience, help your child think about what needs to be taken into account when writing for that audience.

Kaia's (and My!) Story (continued)

My brewing research paper crisis led to a valiant attempt by the school librarian, Ms. Nelson, to help me. Ms. Nelson was kind and compassionate, and she was also good friends with Mrs. Longo. One day, Ms. Nelson pulled me aside and said, "Daniel, you have to write something for your research class. Mrs. Longo doesn't want to fail you. If you write anything and turn it in, she'll give you a D. But you have to write something for her to give you a D."

Knowing I loved sports and history, Ms. Nelson pulled a book off the shelf and said, "Daniel, jai alai is a fascinating sport. It has ancient origins and requires excellent athleticism." She opened the book and read a couple pages out loud to me. "Write something, anything, about jai alai so Mrs. Longo doesn't have to flunk you." I said, "Okay, I will." But I didn't. I couldn't. Eventually, the last day of class arrived, and I didn't have a single word to give Mrs. Longo. I failed her class.

To this day, I still think about how much it would have pleased me to have penned a magnificent piece for Mrs. Longo. It certainly wasn't my ambition to get an F. Without a drop of uncertainty, I can tell you that the hundreds of underperforming students I have worked with would have loved to have been A students too. These students are never doing poorly because they want to. They are challenged by circumstances beyond their control and need help to get on track.

I can only imagine how different Mrs. Longo's class would have been for me if the support I needed had been available. I feel certain I would have been able to produce a respectable paper if someone had broken down the assignment for me step by step, talked me through each task, and helped me whenever I got stuck. I was unbelievably lucky to have had the support of Ms. Nelson, but I needed so much more than encouragement. What I needed was someone constantly by my side, mentoring me through the entire process.

Kaia's (and My!) Story (continued)

When I approached my work with Kaia, I remembered my own experience. I wished I'd had a mentor, and that's what I wanted to be for her. I studied her writing assignment. I carefully dissected the requirements to make sure I completely understood every facet of the assignment. Then I broke it down into step-by-step tasks, and Kaia and I drafted timelines for getting each task done. Approaching my work with Kaia in this way allowed her to not only produce an excellent research paper but also learn critical writing skills.

Writing Five-Paragraph Essays

When writing five-paragraph essays, remind your child that the first paragraph is the introductory paragraph. In addition to a main idea or thesis, an introduction should include a hook, something catchy to bring the reader in. The introduction should also provide the reader with an overview of the topic and purpose. The next three paragraphs address the thesis introduced in the first paragraph. Each paragraph should begin with a topic sentence. The concluding paragraph restates the thesis and wraps up the theme of the essay. It also often includes a "so what?" statement that addresses broader implications.

Show your child how the five-paragraph structure can be used for longer writing assignments. For example, in a research paper comparing the governmental systems of two countries, your child might be required to write five paragraphs on each country. The entire research paper will need a comprehensive introductory paragraph and a comprehensive concluding paragraph.

Proofreading

When your child is finished writing, check his or her work for clarity, thoroughness, and mechanics. Make sure your child followed the teacher's directions. If changes are needed, ask your child how much support he or she would like with revisions. Some children want a high level of independence. Other children welcome help.

Submitting a Writing Assignment

Make sure your child's assignment is ready to submit on the day it is due. Double-check with your child later in the day, before he or she leaves school, that the paper was submitted. If you feel it's necessary, send your child's teacher an email to confirm it was submitted.

Once the entire project is over, help your child appreciate that he or she now has a track record of completing a challenging writing assignment. Follow up with your child when you think the paper will be graded and returned.

Reviewing the Returned Writing Assignment

Carefully read the teacher's notes and discuss the grade with your child. If your child received a lower grade than hoped for, encourage your child to meet with the teacher to find out if there is an opportunity to make corrections and resubmit the paper. Or ask about doing another assignment for extra credit.

Resubmitting work and pursuing extra credit will help raise your child's grades. More importantly, it will demonstrate to your child's teachers that he or she cares about his or her classes. It will also promote your child's sense of responsibility.

Kaia's (and My!) Story (continued)

*It is always magical when a life experience comes full circle,
especially when the outcome is better the second time. This was my
experience working with Kaia. I came face-to-face with a writing
trauma I experienced in high school, but this time I was prepared.
Kaia and I worked together as a team every step of the way. We
talked through everything that needed to be accomplished and strove
to produce the best research paper possible. In the end, Kaia
generated an excellent paper and earned a well-deserved high grade.
More importantly, Kaia learned how to manage all of the demands
of writing a research paper.*

Conclusion

I haven't yet met a child who doesn't want to do well in school, nor have
I yet met a child who isn't disappointed by getting a bad grade. Even with
help, children may not earn good grades. For children with dysgraphia,
receiving a bad grade on a writing assignment often feels doubly discour-
aging. They put in so much effort that when they receive a bad grade, the
time and energy hardly feel worth it. It is up to you to help your child
find value in the process. In time, the results will come. But it does take
a long time, and your child will need your support to stay motivated and
believe his or her efforts have value.

For children with language-based learning difficulties, both reading
and writing will remain a multistep process even as they grow older and
more skilled. You can help your child manage the demands of writing
assignments by planning ahead, helping him or her develop ideas, and
suggesting words and phrases he or she can use. Approaching writing
collaboratively is the best way to manage the demands of writing assignments. More importantly, collaboration is the quickest way to help your
child acquire the writing skills needed to become a skilled writer and a
successful student.

CHAPTER 8

Dyscalculia: Unable to Compute in a STEM World

Children with dyscalculia tend to exhibit challenges in all areas of math, including money, measurement, and time. These challenges not only impact their ability to perform well at school but many crucial life skills as well. For a child with dyscalculia, remedial support will be needed. Surprisingly, a number of the children I have worked with who struggled in all areas of math have gone on to excel in mathematics. It has been my observation that many of the challenges children have with math are resolved with appropriate levels of intervention and maturation.

Many current educational programs feature integrated science, technology, engineering, and math (STEM) curricula. For typical children, the math instruction that is offered through school is usually sufficient to acquire mastery. However, children with dyscalculia need additional support and instruction after school to fully understand what is being taught in class and to complete homework assignments.

In this chapter, you'll learn how to approach math support in a way that will be highly beneficial for your child. I'll help you promote number sense and math fluency. I'll help you tackle word problems and address math anxiety. I'll also share how using *metacognition*, an approach that encourages thinking about thinking, can help children self-correct habitual mistakes.

Although this chapter focuses primarily on the support and development of foundational math skills, many of the approaches to math support I offer will also work well for students in middle school and high school. If you have a teenager, consider reviewing middle school and high school math concepts before partnering on math homework. You might also collaborate with a math specialist or math tutor; encourage the specialist or tutor to incorporate the strategies offered in this chapter.

Creating a Culture of Math in Your Home

Children with dyscalculia and related LBLDs benefit from high levels of explicit instruction in all areas of mathematics. As with all learning difficulties, early identification and early intervention are the best bets for securing a good outcome, but it is never too late to help your child. This is especially true of children with dyscalculia.

There are five keys to success in promoting well-developed math skills in your child:

Provide exposure to math concepts. This can be done in different ways: speaking, listening, and doing. For example, measure your child's height. Then have him or her measure your height. Subtract the heights to get a difference. Add your heights to get a total height. Be creative and find activities that are enjoyable for both of you.

Provide hands-on materials. Also known as *manipulatives*, items such as counting blocks, marbles, checkers, giant dice, and large dominos stimulate the brain and make the brain more open to learning and remembering.

Match the activity to ability. Always adjust activities to a level where your child can be highly successful. Do not introduce a challenge that exceeds your child's capacities. For children with dyscalculia, progress is slow, so be prepared to move at a slow pace, but keep it going.

Look for signs of unease. Some children will enjoy playing math-related games every day for many minutes. Other children may only be able to play these games one or two times a week for just a few minutes at a time. Pay attention to your child. If you notice any signs of anxiety or boredom, dial down or stop what you are doing.

Have fun! Most important, your child needs to enjoy math. Choose math activities that are fun and engaging to help your child build comfort and familiarity with math concepts. The next section offers plenty of strategies for getting playful with numbers.

How to Make Math More Enjoyable

Children with dyscalculia need extra practice and support to master counting and basic number sense, such as the relationship between larger and smaller numbers. These children also require explicit instruction with regard to money, measurements, shapes, and time. The good news is that when we structure additional support and practice in a way that is compatible with a child's learning characteristics, children with dyscalculia can make excellent gains in all of these areas.

Let's look at some of the strategies you can use with your child to master important areas of math. For a handy downloadable checklist of the tips in this chapter, visit this book's website: http://www.newharbin ger.com/40989.

Counting

To help your child develop counting skills and number sense, post a number line with large, easy-to-read numbers in your child's bedroom or play area. Help your child recognize the relationship that numbers have to one another. For instance, you might say, "Four comes before five but after three (3, 4, 5)." Be sure to use familiar objects, such as fingers and toes, to practice counting, and use a rising intonation as you count higher.

Then, help your child understand that every number corresponds to a quantity (3 = ***). This will lead into working on math-related concepts such as money, measurement, and time. For these concepts, you can use real-life examples to reinforce direct instruction.

As your child becomes more proficient in counting, engage in basic adding and subtracting games. Start by using actual objects. You can also purchase inexpensive large dice and create a game of rolling dice and adding the numbers or, conversely, rolling the dice and subtracting the numbers.

Teach your child to count by 2s, 3s, 4s, 5s, 6s, 7s, 8s, 9s, and 10s when he or she is ready. You might want to start with 2s, 5s, and 10s. Help your child recognize that multiplication is just another way of adding ($3 \times 4 = 4 + 4 + 4$).

Money

To help your child learn about money, begin by teaching him or her how to recognize the value of coins and bills. You can play simple addition and subtraction games using whatever you have on hand. You can also play "shopkeeper." Provide your child with a number of different coins and bills, and have him or her play the role of shopkeeper or customer. Pretend to buy or sell imaginary items. Switch places. When you are at a store, teach your child where to find prices of merchandise.

Help your child learn about the value of saving money by starting a savings jar. As the parent, choose how much money is contributed and how often. But if you are able, let your child choose what will be done with the money saved. You don't need to use large amounts of money; even contributing one quarter a week will allow your child to see that it can take several weeks to save enough money to buy a pack of gum or donate enough money to cover the cost of a meal at a shelter.

Measurement

To help your child learn about measurement, engage in relatable measuring activities: find the height of friends and family members, find the width and length of your child's bedroom, and follow recipes. Encouraging your child to cook with you and engaging in conversations about the ingredients you are using and why you are using specific amounts will give your son or daughter experience counting, measuring, and learning about ratios. As your child's math skills improve, you can double or halve a recipe to try new calculations.

Use a variety of tools when measuring, such as rulers, tape measurers, measuring spoons, cups, and scales. Teach your child about distance, such as miles, by taking your son or daughter on a walk or car ride and letting him or her know when you have traveled one mile. Teach your child about weight by letting him or her use a scale to weigh household objects; describe the concepts of pounds, ounces, and kilograms. If your child is required to calculate the area of a square or rectangle, you can relate this to the area of a soccer field or baseball diamond. If your child is learning about statistics and how to average numbers, attribute a set of numbers to the scores of an athlete. These are all ways to help your child stay engaged.

Shapes

Help your child recognize basic shapes: circles, squares, triangles, and so on. Start by drawing a wide variety of shapes on a large sheet of paper or whiteboard. Have your child say the name of each shape. As your child is able to identify shapes easily, move on to three-dimensional shapes such as spheres (balls), cubes (blocks), and columns (straws).

As your child gets older, discuss the concepts of perimeter, area, and volume in ways your child can relate to, such as the amount of carpet needed to cover a floor or how much water is in a fish tank.

Time

Use an analog clock to help your child learn time. Analog clocks are better than digital clocks for learning time because it is easier for a child to recognize the relationship between seconds, minutes, and hours. Have your child count to sixty so he or she experiences one minute. You can also time your child while he or she runs from one side of a playground to the other side to teach about measuring time.

Teach your child that there are twenty-four hours in a day. Explain that he or she is at school for about seven hours and that he or she sleeps for about eight or nine hours.

Using a calendar, help your child understand the relationships between days, weeks, months, years, and decades. Help your child use a calendar on a regular basis to reinforce how time is used and passes by.

How to Introduce Metacognition (Thinking About Thinking)

Few things are more enjoyable than helping students discover individualized strategies that help them succeed. *Metacognition*—the process of thinking about your own thinking—is one strategy that can be very effective in getting children with dyscalculia to correct a mistake they make frequently. Mathematics by its very nature benefits from a thought process that involves questioning, so there are plenty of opportunities for your child to practice thinking about his or her own thinking while doing math-related activities. When we systematically promote the use of metacognition in children of all ages, we provide them with a useful learning strategy.

Jason's story is an example of how even a very young child can learn about metacognition and benefit from it.

• *Jason's Story*

Jason was an extremely clever, creative, and energetic second-grader. Despite a fairly optimal school environment, his written language skills were emerging slowly and with great difficulty, which was not uncommon for children his age. These challenges were spilling over into other areas. For example, when I first began working with him, I evaluated his ability to write the numbers 1 through 20. First, I had him write 1 to 10. This first attempt was challenging, and he reversed the direction of many numbers.

Many children struggle with number reversals—whether they have dyscalculia or not. Here (and also on this book's website, http://www .newharbinger.com/40989) are steps to help with this common problem.

How to Correct Number Reversals

Reversals of numbers can be cleared up quite quickly by taking a few simple steps. We'll use the number 3 as an example.

1. First, provide an example of what a 3 looks like. Point out how the number 3 points left, not right, as with an E.

2. Next, write a correct version of 3 and then have your child replicate it three more times.

3. After that, provide your child with a blank sheet of paper. Ask your child what direction the 3 should point. Make sure he or she points to the left. This is a metacognitive strategy in action because you are asking your child to think before writing.

4. Finally, have your child write a 3 without a reference.

5. About five to ten minutes later, ask your child if he or she is ready to make another 3. Use the metacognitive strategy again by reminding your child to think about the direction the number needs to point. Then have him or her practice making a 3 one more time.

Jason's Story (continued)

When we began to work on the numbers 12 through 19, Jason found it virtually impossible not to transpose the numerals. Twelve became 21 and 13 became 31. What was immediately evident to me was that when he heard the number 13, his brain registered the 3 first, which compelled him to write the 3 before the 1.

I said, "I am going to teach you a grown-up word, a word you are not expected to know. The word is 'metacognition.'" I asked Jason to repeat the word. With some effort, he was able to say it. I explained what metacognition was and said, "We are going to use metacognition to address an area that has been a little bit challenging for you."

We talked about how the number 12 seems to start with the number 2, and the number 13 seems to start with the number 3, and the number 14 seems to start with the number 4—and that it was understandable that this created a challenge. I then explained that these numbers are actually written differently from how they sound. We then discussed how metacognition would help him correctly form the numbers 12 through 19. For several weeks, we would write the *numbers 1 through 11, stop, discuss the meaning of the word "metacognition" and talk about how he was going to think about his thinking before forming the numbers 12 through 19. Although at first he occasionally transposed the numerals, in very short order he consistently got it right.*

If your child is transposing numbers, you can use the same steps to correct the habit as if it were a reversal of numbers. The exercise below is also available for download on this book's website, http://www.newhar binger.com/40989.

How to Correct the Transposing of Numbers

Take these steps when your child incorrectly writes the sequence of numbers, for example, writing 41 when the intended number is 14.

1. First, provide an example of what 14 looks like. Point out how the number 1 comes before the number 4.

2. Next, copy your version of 14 and then have him or her copy it three more times.

3. After that, provide your child with a blank sheet of paper. Ask your child what number in the pair comes first. Make sure he or she says 1. This is a metacognitive strategy in action because you are asking your child to think before he or she does any writing.

4. Finally, have your child write a 14 without a reference.

5. About five to ten minutes later, ask your child if he or she is ready to make another 14. Use the metacognitive strategy again by reminding your child to think about what number should come first. Then have him or her practice making a 14 one more time.

How to Supplement Math

Balance the amount of additional math instruction you provide with the amount of math instruction your child is getting at school. In general, aim to supplement your child's math instruction every two or three days, but be careful not to add to your child's sense of frustration or futility. Remember that these activities should reinforce learning without challenging your child beyond his or her capacities.

It is better to work with your child frequently for shorter bursts of time than it is to have one long session per week. One or two minutes of flashcards or a math game counts. You will be the best judge in determining the length of time to work with your child. If your child is really enjoying the process, longer sessions are fine.

It's okay to take breaks from supplemental math instruction too. A few weeks without math over the summer or during school breaks is fine.

Math Fluency

As a parent, one of the most helpful things you can do for your child with dyscalculia is to improve his or her *math fluency*. Math fluency is very similar to reading fluency in that it allows a student to swiftly analyze a math problem and know which strategies to apply for arriving at a solution. The main benefit of math fluency is that it frees up a child's brain so that he or she is able to learn and work on higher-order math problems.

To promote math fluency, it is important for children to engage in a lot of repetition. Repetitive math problems that are within a child's capacity are very motivating. Children with dyscalculia have less experience engaging in basic arithmetic problems. Therefore, it is essential for parents to provide additional practice and reinforcement in all foundational math skills.

Promoting math fluency begins by engaging your child in activities that rely on skills that he or she already has. Strive to get a sense of your child's math ability level. Is he or she able to add single-digit numbers but not two-digit numbers? If this is the case, then do a lot of math problems with single-digit numbers.

I'm a big fan of mad-minute math worksheets (see http://www.web mathminute.com/sheets.asp for just one of many sources on the Internet) to promote fluency in the areas of addition, subtraction, multiplication, and division. Try to have your child complete one mad-minute worksheet three or four days a week, but adjust the number of problems to fit easily within your child's capacities. Always keep the challenge level well within your child's skill range. Only increase the level when your child is totally capable of completing a sheet with considerable ease.

How to Help with Math Homework

As your child's study partner, teaching and reinforcing math concepts will be paramount. But if you find that you cannot explain math assignments in a way your child easily understands, don't worry. Do the parts of the assignment that are easy for the two of you to do, then write a note to your child's teacher explaining that your child did not understand the uncompleted portion.

Keep it positive. It's critical that you don't allow the homework experience to be frustrating for your child or you. Feelings of frustration about learning and schoolwork can make a bad situation worse. It is important to prevent your child from developing negative feelings about him or herself as a learner and about learning in general.

Stay calm. Because children are exquisitely sensitive to their parent's state of mind, it is essential that you project a calm demeanor. I know this can be a tall order when faced with challenging math assignments. I recommend you take the following steps to become more comfortable with your child's math homework:

- Carefully review your child's math homework. If needed, make a photocopy of the assignment, and complete some or all of the assignment yourself in advance.

- While completing the assignment, consider the instructional strategies or resources you might want to use that will help your child better understand the concepts.

- Once you are entirely comfortable with the assignment, have your child join you. Explain to your child what the key learning objective is while completing the homework. A key objective might be learning to borrow while doing subtraction problems, or it might be to simply get quicker at doing math computations like adding, subtracting, multiplying, or dividing.

- Ask your child to choose a problem to solve and work on it together. Continue allowing your child to choose the problems he or she wants to work on.

- If your child is reluctant or resists working on math homework, ask him or her to identify one or two math problems for you to do. Embrace the task and do the problems with some joy and flourish to communicate your optimism and comfort with the task. Your mindset will become your child's. Then ask your child if there's a problem anywhere on the page that he or she would like to try. Remember, math problems do not need to be done in sequence; they just need to be done. They will be done quicker and with better learning outcomes if you approach math assignments this way.

Don't overdo it. Frequently teachers will assign twenty to forty math problems for homework. For many children with LBLDs, this is simply too much. Although there is value in repetition as a means of developing math fluency, students with LBLDs usually run out of steam long before they are able to complete all of the assigned problems. Evaluate how much you feel your child is capable of doing. Help your child appreciate that he or she only has to do a few of the math problems.

Ensure clarity of concepts. Look at the math assignment. Start by helping your child determine whether he or she understands the concepts. Math homework is typically a review of the day's teaching or a review of previously taught concepts. However, for many children with LBLDs, what the teacher thinks of as review material can actually be unfamiliar and challenging to your child. It's possible your child does not understand the concepts contained in the assignments, and he or she may require significant reteaching. This is yet another reason why it is so critical to be highly involved in your child's homework completion.

Set a time limit. Decide together on an amount of time you will spend working on math, and try to keep within that time frame. If your child decides to work longer because he or she seems to be enjoying the work, continue.

Work within your child's capacity. There may be days when almost all of the math assignment will exceed your child's skill level. When this happens, narrow your focus to doing only what is reasonable given your child's capacities. This may mean that you spend your entire math time working on a single problem. That's okay. It might take several days or perhaps several weeks for your child to master a new skill being taught in math.

Bypass Strategies for Math and Science Assignments

If you need to work around your child's language-based learning disability, you can find additional tips by visiting this book's website: http://www .newharbinger.com/40989. There, you'll find numerous ways to bypass your child's slowly emerging math skills so that he or she can ultimately learn what is expected.

Troubleshooting Common Math Homework Problems

Part of making math homework manageable for your child will be understanding how to help in three areas where problems tend to arise: *transcription*; *calculation errors*, which are often called "careless mistakes"; and *word problems*.

Transcription

Sometimes students are expected to transcribe math problems from their textbooks onto a worksheet and show their work. For children with LBLDs, this can be extremely challenging. It is a classic case of *subskill coupling* (see chapter 3 for a refresher on this term). The inability to accurately transcribe the math problem makes it nearly impossible to practice the math concept. The key to success in this case is scaffolding the tasks so that your child can focus on the primary learning objective, which is practicing math skills. You may need to assist with the transcription part of the assignment to prevent writing from expending all of your child's energy. If you don't, he or she will not have enough energy left over for the actual math work. I also recommend that you use graph paper to help your child accurately line up numbers while showing his or her work.

Calculation Errors

When children make a calculation error, it is often called a "careless mistake." There are no careless mistakes! "Careless" implies there is no care, but a child who does his or her homework *does* care. It's not helpful to characterize a child as careless or lazy or anything else negative. To promote your child's growth mindset, rephrase the nature of these mistakes. You can point out to your child, "You care so much about completing your work that you missed a step."

Calculation errors are usually caused by the inability to slow down sufficiently to confirm that every step in a procedure has been completed correctly. To help your child slow down, remind him or her at the outset that, when doing math, speed works against us; taking our time is our greatest ally. To encourage a slower pace, ask your child to explain each step as he or she does it and to confirm what will be done next. The capacity to solve each component of a math problem slowly enough to avoid making these mistakes emerges over time.

Once your child has mastered a math concept, it is okay to allow him or her to work quickly—as long as it is not at the expense of accuracy. There may even come a time when your child can do the computation in his or her head quickly. That's great. This is how we build math fluency, which is critical to acquire more advanced math skills.

Word Problems

Word problems are especially challenging for children with language-based learning difficulties. Work closely with your child to read the word problem and explain what it says. Help your child learn how to convert a word problem into a numeric problem by using diagrams and other manipulatives.

Use checkers, marbles, or other sets of items if the word problem involves grouping objects. You may even create stick figures and show how one stick figure character, Lisa, has ten cookies, and her friend, Arnold, has four cookies; then your child can see from this illustration how a word problem is converted into a pictograph that is then converted into a numeric problem: $10 + 4 = 14$.

How to Manage Math Anxiety

Children with dyscalculia are more prone to math anxiety than other children. The catch-22 with math anxiety is that these children are less likely to engage in math-related activities, and therefore they fall farther behind their peers in math skill development. Falling behind exacerbates a child's level of anxiety, which in turn diminishes his or her desire to engage in mathematics. And so it goes.

A child's comfort with math is often proportional to that of his or her parent's comfort with math. As your child's study partner, you will need to become comfortable with basic math and present a positive attitude toward the subject. If you embrace an appreciation for math, your child will too.

Let your child know that learning math is a process and takes time. Let him or her know you will always be there to help with math for as long as he or she needs you.

Many children with dyscalculia develop anxiety because they believe their teachers view their poor performance or learning pace as a result of not trying hard enough. These children can quickly become acutely anxious, making it harder to learn in class and then harder to perform well on homework and tests. Here are some ways to put your child at ease in this regard:

- Let your child's math teacher know that your son or daughter has dyscalculia, and establish good communication with this teacher.

- Strive to provide your child with as much pre-teaching as possible so that when your child arrives at class, he or she will have an understanding of what is being taught.

- Ask your child's teacher to provide your child with fewer and easier math problems when doing seatwork. Some teachers are willing to circle just a few problems on a worksheet for a child to do. This is subtle and does not take much time on the part of the teacher.

Jason's story (continued)

I was conducting a presentation for a small group of teachers at Jason's school when I happened to see Jason walk past just as I was discussing metacognition. Knowing that he enjoyed an audience, I waved him into the room and asked if he wanted to explain what the word "metacognition" means. "Thinking about thinking," he stated proudly. Among the group of teachers there were several audible gasps of surprise and delight, which were followed by a great round of applause. This brought an immense smile to Jason's face, and he continued on his way almost certainly happier, prouder, and more confident in himself and his ability to learn.

Conclusion

Dyscalculia is a common and challenging learning difficulty for many children. Fortunately, there are many things you as a parent can do to help minimize the detrimental impact it has on your child's learning, skills development, and self-esteem. By taking a highly proactive role, you can cultivate a culture of math in your home and jump-start your child's math learning.

In addition, you can provide crucial math support by staying apprised of your child's math learning needs at school, actively participating in math homework completion, and providing your child with a reasonable amount of supplementary math instruction to boost his or her math skills.

Finally, I encourage you to introduce your child to the concept of metacognition. If it can help Jason, it may certainly help your child!

CHAPTER 9

Information Processing and Memory

Two areas where children with language-based learning difficulties can be significantly impacted are *auditory processing* (more specifically, *spoken language processing*) and *visual processing*. In this chapter, when I address spoken "language processing" and "visual processing" issues, I am not referring to deficits in hearing or seeing, but rather *the capacity to process, understand, and remember information received by listening to spoken language or by seeing*. This is an important distinction, because many individuals who have been identified as having spoken language processing deficits are extraordinary musicians with a remarkable ear for all kinds of sound and sound relationships. In a similar vein, many individuals who have been identified as having visual processing deficits are extraordinary artists. They have a remarkable sense of line, shape, form, color, and spatial relationships that is critical for all forms of artwork. The problem these individuals experience with spoken language and visual processing is not a function of their hearing or vision, but rather a function of the means by which information—specifically spoken language and visual information—is processed, stored, and retrieved.

Accurate spoken language processing and visual processing place enormous demands on children with LBLDs. These children are already overwhelmed by distractions, have a shortage of working memory, and have underdeveloped strategies for effectively processing information they hear and see. Fortunately, there is a lot you can do to help your child if he or she has slowly emerging information processing skills.

Reading and writing challenges are relatively easy to identify. Determining if a child has delays in spoken language or visual processing is more difficult. Pay close attention to your child's ability: If you notice that you have to repeat directions several times or slow down your delivery of directions, your child might have spoken language processing delays. If visual tasks such as putting together puzzles, recognizing differences between objects, and understanding maps and diagrams are exceptionally challenging for your child, he or she might have visual processing delays.

Do not be alarmed if you detect that your child struggles in these areas. Moderate delays in processing information are common for children with LBLDs. Your support might be enough to help your child manage the demands of school and homework despite his or her processing difficulties.

If you are concerned that your child's capacities in these areas are significantly delayed, it might be beneficial to seek a consultation with an audiologist or vision expert. If the expert recommends a treatment regimen for your child, gather as much information as you can about the condition the clinician has identified, and carefully vet prospective providers of any treatment that was recommended. For a list of important considerations when reviewing the treatment recommendations of an audiologist or vision expert, see this book's website: http://www.newhar binger.com/40989.

In general, leading experts in special education recommend that efforts to improve spoken language and visual processing capacities be integrated with activities that involve academic skill development. In other words, treating information processing deficits in a way that has no direct relationship to broader areas of learning is unproductive (Fletcher et al. 2007).

In this chapter, you'll learn strategies that will enhance your child's processing capacities and memory by engaging him or her in learning-related activities. Most of these strategies combine both spoken language and visual approaches to process, remember, and retrieve information. These strategies apply to all areas of learning and can enhance your child's memory and retrieval skills even if he or she does not have a significant delay in spoken language or visual processing.

Nuts and Bolts of Memory

Many children with LBLDs struggle to understand what their teachers are saying during class. These children can also be challenged by the vast amount of content that is presented through visual means, as in pictures, illustrations, and diagrams. Whether receiving information through listening or seeing, your child will be unable to remember what is being taught if he or she has not accurately processed the information.

Memory is fundamental to learning. But individual differences in *how* any given child remembers best are not always taken into account. Throughout this book, I urge parents to become experts on their child's learning characteristics, and a critical area of your expertise is understanding how your child remembers best. As a parent of a child with an LBLD, you will find it useful to fill your teaching toolbox with as many strategies as you can to promote memory of what is taught at school. Here are strategies to help you acquire these important tools.

Providing Your Child with Consolidation Time

Children with LBLDs frequently need more time than their peers to process what they are taught. Much of what they hear and see during class passes by so quickly that they are unable to understand and remember it. As your child's study partner, you can help make up some of what was missed by revisiting concepts while doing homework.

As you work with your child on homework assignments, identify content critical for your child to learn. Working one-on-one with your child will allow you to present material at a rate that is compatible with his or her capacity to process information. Be thoughtful about the rate at which you present material and how quickly you move from one concept to the next. If you move too quickly to a new concept, the initial concept may not be adequately processed and retained.

To understand how we process and remember information, picture an hourglass. We are all familiar with the slow trickle of sand that drains from the top down to the bottom through the narrow middle. Now, imagine the top of the hourglass is your short-term memory, sometimes called *working memory*. Any information we receive is first held in our short-term memory, the top of the hourglass. Over time, this information is transferred to our long-term memory, the bottom of the hourglass. The space we have for short-term memory is limited. If we receive too much information too quickly, it is as if the top of the hourglass overflows. The sand that spills over the sides is information that is lost. We need to receive information slowly enough to prevent overflowing.

You can help your child by carefully considering how much information he or she is capable of processing at any given time. This will help you gauge how much information you want to present to him or her. In addition, it's also important to take pauses when delivering information in order to allow the information that's being held in short-term memory to trickle into long-term memory.

Be alert to when your child has an aha moment. Then, wait a minute or two before moving on to a new concept so that your child can adequately cement what he or she just learned. If you present more information without a pause, everything that he or she has just grasped will "spill out" of short-term memory. I call these critical pauses *consolidation time* because they provide a child time to consolidate what he or she is learning.

After an aha moment, it can sometimes be helpful to play a couple of games of tic-tac-toe or Go Fish, or engage in some other fun activity like drawing or putting together a puzzle. The time spent engaged in these activities is just what your child's brain needs to process and store what he or she has just learned (Aamodt and Wang 2011).

Memory: What Goes in Needs to Come Out

When it comes to memory, the ability to store information is only half of the story. The other equally important half is retrieval. *It is actually the retrieval of information that strengthens our capacity to remember what was taught.*

Some years ago, I came across an hourglass that was filled halfway with water and halfway with blue oil. I used this unique hourglass to illustrate another memory principle to my students. As we all know, oil floats in water. Once the hourglass is flipped over, the oil appears to defy gravity and rise up from the bottom half, which represents long-term memory. The oil then flows into the top globe, which represents working (short-term) memory. It is this back-and-forth process of information going into long-term memory and then being retrieved and going into working memory that promotes memory. As a parent, you can systematically reinforce this process of retrieval.

More than a century ago, German psychologist and memory expert Hermann Ebbinghaus studied the phenomenon of forgetting. He discovered that if someone is asked to retrieve information immediately after receiving it, the person is likely to accurately and completely retrieve that information. If there is a significant delay between receiving information and retrieving it, there tends to be a decrease in both the accuracy and quantity of information that can be retrieved.

It is important to allow this phenomenon to inform your approach to helping your child better remember what he or she is taught. When you are teaching your child a new concept, systematically increase the amount of time between each retrieval of information. For example, provide your child with a definition of a word and then immediately ask him or her to repeat the definition. Then allow thirty seconds to elapse before again asking your child to recall the information. Then allow a minute or two to elapse, and again ask your child to recall the information. If your child provides the correct answer, stretch out the recall time to five or ten minutes, and then to thirty minutes or an hour. Build up the recall time to several hours and eventually a day or two. By systematically increasing the amount of time between retrievals, you will improve your child's memory of the concepts you are teaching. For a child with spoken language and visual processing delays, this method is essential because of inefficiencies he or she may experience in processing information as it comes in.

Motivation and Memory

Motivation expert Daniel Pink has identified three key ingredients of motivation: *autonomy* (a high degree of freedom and choice), *purpose* (knowing why something is being done), and *mastery* (being successful).

Leveraging these key ingredients when helping your child study and memorize information can make studying more productive.

You can promote your child's *autonomy* by letting him or her choose the approach used to remember material. You can encourage your child's sense of *purpose* by helping him or her appreciate why it's important to remember the material. Help your child recognize the many ways he or she will benefit from making an effort to study and learn; if good grades incentivize your child, remind him or her how the extra effort can result in an improved grade. You can promote your child's sense of *mastery* by working together in a proactive way, using the study tips throughout this book.

Strategies to Help Your Child Process and Remember

There are many fun and interesting ways to help your child remember material he or she is expected to learn. The strategies that follow are ones I have used over the years to help my students with LBLDs to better process and retain things they are being taught and to effectively prepare for tests and quizzes. It is my hope that you will identify strategies that are compatible with the way your child learns best and to take into account any challenges he or she has with spoken language and visual processing.

Be a source of calm. Children with LBLDs are frequently anxious and distracted while in the classroom—and therefore they cannot efficiently process and remember what they hear and see. Your child is more likely to be calm and emotionally regulated when you are in a similar state. By helping your child be calm and regulated, you can help him or her accurately process and remember information missed during class.

Prime your child before studying begins. The more prepared your child is to take in information, the more successful he or she will be at retaining it. For example, if your child is studying for a comprehensive U.S. government exam that includes knowing the Bill of Rights, you might say to your child before beginning any work, "We are going to review the Bill of Rights. What is the Bill of Rights?" You would want your child to say, "The Bill of Rights is the first ten amendments in the Constitution." If your child struggles to accurately recall the information correctly, be sure to immediately provide clarification and then restate your question.

Begin and end homework with the most important points. We tend to remember the first and last things we experience. For example, it's often easy to remember arriving at a destination and leaving a destination, but events in the middle are sometimes more difficult to recall. As a parent, you can leverage this phenomenon when helping your child study for a test by beginning and ending your study session with the most important concepts.

Infuse content with emotion. All people process and remember information better if they have an emotional connection to it. Your child is more likely to remember important details about what he or she is learning if he or she feels strongly about the material. For example, if you are helping your child learn something about Colonial America, you might want to relay an anecdote about an especially heroic person or some great tragedy that occurred during this time. The emotion that these stories evoke will promote the memory of all the related content.

Make content relevant. Relevance is relative, especially for children. The important things your child needs to learn will only seem relevant to him or her if they seem relevant to you. As a parent, find a genuine interest in the content you are trying to teach your child. The topic of photosynthesis might not be entirely exciting to you, but if you can find some excitement in it, it will help your child. Your excitement will become your child's excitement, and he or she will be better able to learn about photosynthesis.

Connect the new with the old. Help your child make an association between what he or she already knows and the new information you are teaching. This will improve your child's ability to remember the material. One way to do this is to connect new information to a familiar image, helping your child visualize what you are teaching. For example, use the familiar image of a bicycle wheel to help your child "see" the stages of the water cycle. You can also connect new information to a familiar word. Your child probably knows that the word "ignite" means to catch fire. Help him or her connect the word "ignite" to the word "igneous" when learning about the class of rocks formed from lava. Word associations like this are enormously helpful.

Take complexity into account. When explaining concepts to your child, only go into the degree of complexity you feel your child is capable of understanding, and eliminate extraneous information. For example, it's possible your child does not need to understand how atoms combine to make molecules to know that photosynthesis is how plants produce food for themselves. Stick to the learning objective, and keep the information streamlined.

Match the study location to what is being studied. Our capacity for memory grew out of our need to navigate the physical world: in order to find food, water, shelter, and friends, we needed to be able to navigate the environment. We can leverage this natural capacity to remember details in our environment by connecting what we are learning with physical reference points. For example, if you are helping your child prepare for an anatomy exam covering the digestive system, you might want to study in your kitchen; you can more easily connect how things in that room, such as food and cookware, correspond to aspects of the digestive system. You could relate structural components of your house, such as beams and walls, to the skeletal system.

Check to make sure your child fully understands a concept. Children frequently overestimate how well they know something. In order for a child to remember something, he or she needs to understand what it means. That is why it is critical to check the depth of your child's understanding by asking him or her to provide you with detailed explanations based on the assignment. For example, if your child has an upcoming quiz on photosynthesis, he or she might feel that simply knowing that photosynthesis is how plants make the food they need for growing is sufficient. You, however, might be aware that for your child to receive full credit on the quiz, he or she will need to know that photosynthesis is a process by which plants use sunlight to combine carbon dioxide with water to produce glucose and oxygen.

Creatively break down difficult words and concepts. Sometimes it can be helpful to take an important word or concept and create playful variations of the term to promote your child's memory of it. For example, you can draw a thermos with the word "hot" on it and water squirting out of the top as a means of helping your child remember that a hydrothermal vent spews superheated water. This approach allows your child to use visual cues to remember the meaning of a word.

Try exaggerated pronunciation. Exaggerated mouth movements and pronunciation enhance memory. This approach is especially good for learning to spell certain words. The word "schedule," for example, can be challenging to spell. Pronouncing it as "skeh-du-lee" makes the spelling easier to remember.

Use exaggerated intonation. Try to change the emphasis you put on words when presenting concepts to your child. If you are describing the water cycle, for example, you might say, "The *hot* sun evaporates the water, which *rises* and then *cools* to form clouds that produce rain, which *falls* back down to the Earth." You could emphasize the word "hot" so it sounds hot. You might say "rises" with a rising intonation, and you might say the word "cools" in a lower, deeper voice, perhaps shivering just a bit.

Incorporate song, rhythm, and melody. Some children are especially good at remembering information if they can put it into a song or melody. A colleague of mine helped her third-grade students learn about adaptation with a catchy song: "Adaptation, adaptation, changes in the body to fit a location."

Use mnemonics, acronyms, and acrostics. A *mnemonic* is a pattern of letters, ideas, or associations that facilitates memory. Children are immensely creative and enjoy coming up with mnemonics. The *acronym* "HOMES" is a great mnemonic for remembering the names of the Great Lakes: Huron, Ontario, Michigan, Erie, and Superior. An *acrostic* is a poem, word puzzle, or other composition in which certain letters in each line form a word or words. An especially creative student of mine came up with the following sentence: "He never ate Kellogg's except when he ran." This helped him remember the noble gases in the order they appear on the periodic table: He (Helium) Never (Neon) Ate (Argon) Kellogg's (Krypton) eXcept (Xenon) when he Ran (Radon)."

Use diagrams. Diagrams are a great way to process and understand important concepts. For example, to help your child learn the three branches of the U.S. government, create a large poster containing a tree with three main branches. One branch would be the executive branch; make a big "X" to help your child remember "executive" and then you might turn the "X" into a figure that represents the president. For the judicial branch, you can make nine stick figures and write the name of a Supreme Court justice your child learned about while studying with you. (I once worked with an eighth-grader who was delighted to learn about Sandra Day O'Connor, who was not only female but also loved to ride horses, just as my student did. Creating this special connection helped my student better remember the judicial branch.) Have your child write an email to his or her senator or congressperson. This process, especially if he or she gets a reply, will create a strong connection between your child and these individuals, thereby strengthening his or her memory of the legislative branch.

Create timelines. Timelines leverage our brain's natural tendency to remember things in sequence. This is what allows us to remember the letters of the alphabet and consecutive numbers. Most people remember events best when they can conjure up a visual recreation of what occurred. Create a long timeline with very simple pictographs and illustrations to help your child visualize the people, events, locations, and other important details that occurred in a story or during an important historical event.

Utilize passive exposure to material. Even familiarizing your child with information in informal ways, such as on a wall poster, increases memory and retention. Identify key words, ideas, and other content your child needs to commit to memory. As a test or quiz approaches, cover the walls of your child's study area with this information. This passive exposure to information will help with memory.

Leverage multiple senses. Sometimes, utilizing as many senses as possible can promote memory. For instance, it is often easy to remember that you have locked your car door when you have the experience of pressing the locking device, watching the lock go down, and hearing the sound your car makes when it locks. The combination of touch, sight, and sound enhances your memory of what occurred. Utilize this knowledge when helping your child remember academic material. For example, while describing plate tectonics, explain the phenomenon, show your child illustrations and videos depicting it, and have him or her physically tear a piece of paper in half and push the two pieces together to represent converging plates. The more your child can physically manipulate objects with his or her hands, the more likely he or she will remember the topic.

Study while walking with your child. Because physical movement promotes memory, sometimes it is helpful to study while moving. Take a walk somewhere peaceful with your child and discuss material that he or she is trying to learn. Avoid movement that requires a great deal of attention, such as one-on-one basketball, because it will be virtually impossible to stay focused on the study material. Simply dribbling a basketball or practicing free throws, however, might work well. Use your own good judgment about what activity will work best for your child.

Avoid sense competition. Vision and sound can compete with one another. Some children with language-based learning disabilities process and remember information better if they can close their eyes while listening to you read. In fact, if you are reading aloud an especially important section from a textbook, encourage your child to close his or her eyes and focus on the words you are saying.

Study Strategies That Promote Memory

You can help your child develop good study habits that also promote information retention. Visit this book's website, http://www.newharbinger .com/40989, for additional tips on helping your child process, retain, and recall information.

Why We Forget

To help your child remember, it is useful to understand how and why we forget in the first place. Psychology professor Peter Vishton, from the College of William and Mary, has identified four reasons we forget.

- **Failure to Encode (lack of understanding)**

  Problem: Your child does not process and understand what he or she is taught.

  Solution: Immediately check for understanding and provide clarification.

- **Decay (quickly forgetting)**

  Problem: Your child quickly forgets what he or she is taught.

  Solution: Employ repetition and recall.

- **Retroactive and Proactive Interference (distractions)**

  Problem: Your child is distracted by something he or she experienced immediately before or immediately after being taught a concept.

  Solution: Identify a very specific learning objective. Try to avoid exposing your child to significant distractions immediately before or immediately after presenting the targeted concept.

- **Timing of the Forgetting Process (insufficient reviewing of material)**

  Problem: Your child forgets what he or she is taught after a day or two.

  Solution: Strategically distribute studying over ever increasing periods of time.

Conclusion

Many children with LBLDs struggle to efficiently process what they see and hear. Not only are these children challenged by the processing of this information, but they are also challenged by the requirement that they memorize it. The more your child remembers, the better at remembering he or she will become. It is a skill that will build on itself as long as you continue to actively foster its development.

CHAPTER 10

Managing ADHD and Executive Functioning Deficits

The skills we need to get things done, from planning a family vacation to managing a household, are called *executive functioning skills*. These are the same skills required of your child to manage the demands of school. They include attention, effort, memory, organization, time management, and many other capacities. For children with ADHD, these capacities are significantly delayed, even into early adulthood (Brown 2005). In chapter 1 of this book, I describe why language-based learning difficulties are best understood as a continuum of learning difficulties that are frequently found together. ADHD is no exception. Not only do we find that children diagnosed with ADHD are frequently diagnosed with dyslexia, but we also find that children diagnosed with dyslexia are frequently diagnosed with ADHD. Because there is pronounced overlap of these two learning difficulties, ADHD is an essential topic to address in a book on parenting a child with LBLDs. In fact, virtually all of the strategies offered throughout this book work well for students with ADHD *and* dyslexia.

In addition to this common overlap, the challenges children with dyslexia have managing the demands of written language (and at times mathematics) are similar to the challenges children with ADHD have with written language and mathematics, in many respects. Whereas underlying weaknesses in written language skills impact children with dyslexia, it is underlying weaknesses in attention, sustained effort, and related capacities that hinder a child with ADHD from successfully managing the demands of written language and math. For children with dyslexia and ADHD, the outcome is the same: pronounced inefficiency in processing written language and acquiring math skills. In this chapter, I do not discuss the use of medication for ADHD; if you are interested in medication, please seek a medical consultation.

All of us can be challenged in some facets of executive functioning, but individuals who are diagnosed with ADHD have a severe and chronic deficit of executive functioning capacities. If your child has been diagnosed with ADHD or is just overwhelmed by the organizational demands of school, taking a highly proactive, collaborative role will bridge the gap between what your child is able to do and what needs to get done. This approach will help your child manage the demands of school *and* acquire essential executive functioning skills, because your child will be learning them in an authentic context—that is, while actually managing real demands. This is a productive way to promote executive functioning skills. A number of studies have shown that many types of computer-based programs designed to improve working memory, critical for executive functioning skills, do not significantly improve real-world capacities such as managing schoolwork (Melby-Lervåg, Redick, and Hulme 2016). For this reason, you are the greatest resource your child has in acquiring these critical executive functioning skills. In time, your child will be able to use these skills with increasing levels of independence.

This chapter will provide you with strategies to help your child maintain organized study areas and backpacks, start assignments, transition from one activity to the next, maintain emotional regulation while completing homework, and manage time. These strategies are also effective for children, teens, and young adults who need help staying organized and budgeting their time—whether they've been diagnosed with ADHD or not. You'll learn how to become your child's teammate to make homework more manageable and perhaps even fun. By doing so, your child will eventually begin to feel more positive about homework because it's completed more efficiently. And when children feel more positive, they also expend greater effort, learn and retain material better, and perform better in school.

Getting (and Staying) Organized

Getting and staying organized requires a broad range of executive functioning skills, time, and energy that your child may or may not have. By routinely engaging in organizational tasks with you, your child will become familiar and comfortable with organizational routines.

Backpacks

Let's start with one of the most common organizational problems students with ADHD have: backpacks. Disorganized backpacks are the root of more school difficulties than you can imagine. One reason an organized backpack is so crucial to school success is the impression it makes on a teacher. When a teacher sees that a student's backpack is not neat, it can send the message to the teacher that the child is not a hard worker. A disorganized backpack also makes it hard for children to quickly locate homework, find the correct folders for each subject, and pull out materials to record assignments.

Many parents have been taught that keeping a backpack organized should be their child's responsibility. Ultimately, it will be, but children, especially those with ADHD, need considerable time, modeling, and instruction to develop all of the capacities that staying organized requires.

• *Lisa's Story*

Lisa was an eighth-grader in an academic free fall. She had a reading disability and ADHD. She enjoyed learning new things, but homework took all the fun out of school for her. In my first session with Lisa, I described to her how people who are successful at their jobs often work in teams. I suggested that having a teammate like me might make homework a little more manageable and perhaps even fun. Lisa was dubious but agreed. "All right, Daniel," she said. "Let's give it a try."

We wasted no time getting started. Having found that a backpack is often the best starting place, I asked Lisa if we could first organize her backpack. Her backpack was in complete disarray. It was filled with old assignments and papers that dated back to the

*beginning of the previous school year. Going through her backpack
and notebooks was like being on an archeological expedition. I
pointed this out to Lisa, and we both laughed.*

*In order to involve her in organizing her backpack, I held up
each sheet of paper and allowed her to decide if it was (a) to be kept
in her backpack, (b) hole-punched and put in a binder, (c) filed
away, or (d) recycled. I did the manual component of organization
for her because I wanted her to focus solely on decision making.*

Modeling is key for children with ADHD. By being your child's
organizer and providing an organizational strategy, you will help your
child learn to take care of him- or herself. Ultimately, your child will
develop a template for what it means to be organized; for the first time,
perhaps, your child will experience what a tidy backpack actually looks
like. This new, neat template, in contrast to the chaotic one, often takes
weeks or months to get the hang of. But once internalized, your child
will be prepared to do the sorting on his or her own.

Workspaces

The process used for keeping your child's backpack orderly can also
be applied to your child's workspace at home. Sit together at your child's
study area at least once a week and work together to make sure all supplies are stocked, trash is cleared, virtual and physical folders and desk-
tops are organized, and required reading materials are accounted for.
Familiarity and repetition with this organizational routine will eventually lead to a habit of neatness.

For more tips on providing organizational support, see this book's
website at http://www.newharbinger.com/40989.

Getting Started on Homework

Just as every car needs an electric starter to turn on its engine, many
children need scaffolding to begin working. It is easy to attribute the
reluctance to start—which is a behavior often associated with ADHD—
to something children have control over, but they do not. Whenever a
child does not start a task independently, you need to get involved.

Work collaboratively with your child to locate his or her backpack, then have your son or daughter bring the backpack to the designated study area. Some days, the best way to get started will be for you to reach into the backpack and take out the required materials. Your child will come to see that the task isn't as daunting as he or she felt it might be once you've actually opened the textbook to the appropriate page, placed the worksheet and pencil on the table, or set up your child's tablet or computer. I find students can actually be enticed into doing homework when an adult reads directions, text, and questions aloud.

By systematically structuring the beginning steps of homework in this way, your child is much more likely to finish the homework assignment. This level of support spares your child the large amounts of energy that starting work independently often requires.

Sustained Attention

At the outset of homework you might find that your child's attention will wane or wander. This is not uncommon in the early stages of homework. Most of us have had the experience that, when beginning to read an article or a book, we have to apply an extra level of effort to get through the first few sentences or paragraphs. A similar phenomenon is true of children while doing homework. It can take a while for your child's brain to become oriented around the task at hand.

Try to keep the discussion lively. Point out interesting facets of the task. Encourage your child to share his or her observations about what you're doing together. In a short while, you will discover that your child's ability to focus on the task at hand will become better. In most instances, children are able to sustain their attention as long as they are enjoying the process and feeling rewarded by it.

A critical facet of promoting sustained attention is supporting your child's working memory. Children with ADHD frequently struggle to effectively juggle a number of different thoughts or concepts simultaneously. You can help your child by providing prompts and reminders concerning important details that are related to the task at hand. You might find it helpful to write out key words on a piece of paper or generate visual cues, such as diagrams and illustrations, that represent concepts your child encounters while working on an assignment. Even if your child's textbook contains illustrations of concepts, by creating your own version of the same diagram, you can engage your child's attention at a higher level. If you feel your child is so inclined, encourage him or her to draw diagrams and illustrations as well. The goal is to help your son or daughter keep in mind critical elements of the topic being covered in a homework assignment. Using this approach is an excellent way to support your child's working memory.

Regulating Emotion During Homework

Children with ADHD frequently have difficulty regulating their emotional state. These children tend to become easily frustrated during challenging tasks, when confused, or when bored. Helping your child maintain the level of emotional regulation required to work productively on homework is dependent on your own emotional state. Children are exquisitely sensitive to the emotional state of their parents; therefore it is critical that you find a place of calm and comfort as you navigate the demands of homework.

One of the most significant challenges all parents contend with while doing homework is their child's feeling of boredom. It is widely acknowledged that boredom is a stressor, and it's been my experience that children with ADHD are especially prone to strong responses out of boredom. As adults, we've developed coping mechanisms for the stress of boredom. Children, however, have not yet fully developed this skill.

If your child is especially susceptible to the detrimental effects of boredom, move through homework tasks as quickly as your child is able. Use good judgment about when to take short exercise breaks to shoot basketball hoops, dance, do a yoga pose, or jump rope. Nothing dissipates stress better than physical activity. You can also move back and forth between academic tasks if you find that that is a successful way to manage your child's stress. While you can provide encouragement and gentle reminders to stay on task, you will best help your child maintain focus and sustained effort by modeling a high level of focus and effort yourself.

Transitions

All of us know the experience of getting comfortable with a task and wanting to stay with it. Once a child acquires some momentum and comfort working on a particular school-related task, he or she may want to stick with it instead of moving on to another homework task. In situations like this, it can be helpful to remind your child that he or she can return to whatever it was that he or she was working on, but that it's important for him or her to shift to another assignment. We can facilitate this transition by taking out the next assignment, for example, the dreaded math worksheet. Once the assignment is in sight, a child is more likely to be willing to transition into it. It might also help for you to put away the work your child has completed as he or she starts the new task. If your child still expresses reluctance to transition, try encouraging him or her to work on the new task for a fixed amount of time, perhaps five to ten minutes.

Although children with ADHD are prone to distraction, it's not uncommon for them to experience a level of hyperfocus that prevents them from shifting their attention appropriately. If your child's hyperfocus seems to be leading to a beneficial outcome, such as writing at great length or generating an incredibly elaborate illustration for an assignment, it might be good to simply allow him or her the time he or she needs to finish. These experiences will undoubtedly be the foundation for sustained attention skills in the future.

If, however, the degree of hyperfocus is so significant that it is at the exclusion of all other things, help your child transition to another activity by first suggesting that he or she work for a few more minutes on the current assignment. Then switch to another activity with the understanding that the new task will only be for a short while. As long as you keep a track record of being true to your word, your child will trust these adjustments and, in time, will acquire the capacities to shift back and forth between high-interest and low-interest activities. The main point here is that it isn't reasonable to expect your child to make transitions while completing homework on his or her own. He or she will need your support and presence at the start of a new activity for transitions to occur smoothly.

Time Management

The need to effectively manage one's time is an essential life skill. Few environments require more attention to careful time management than school. For children and teens with ADHD, the rigorous time structure that school demands is incredibly difficult to deal with.

In time, most children, teens, and young adults with ADHD will develop the capacities to be punctual, establish a reasonable plan to complete homework, study for tests, and submit work on time. While these capacities are developing, however, your child will need a significant amount of support from you.

Throughout this book, I've encouraged you to stay apprised of every facet of your child's schooling demands. Time management is no exception. From simply making it to the bus stop on time to completing a project with a four-week deadline, a child with ADHD desperately needs help. Without time management assistance, these children encounter many setbacks, which only worsens their negative thoughts about themselves as students. This negative self-image can be avoided by following these five simple principles of time management:

1. Think of yourself as the time manager.

2. Make yourself aware of all the important dates and timelines your child is required to adhere to.

3. Create a few visual organizers that are simple, clear, and easy to read: a large month-at-a-glance calendar for school-related matters, posted on a wall in your house; a week-at-a-glance calendar, so your child can visualize what the week will bring; and a day-at-a-glance calendar, so that each morning your son or daughter can visualize what lies ahead for the day.

4. Provide your child with daily reminders about important matters, such as submitting homework assignments.

5. Provide your child with a clock and watch that are easy to read. As your child gets older, teach him or her to recognize the passage of time. Discuss how time is a valuable resource that must be used judiciously.

All this being said, make sure your child also has opportunities to *not* be worried about time. Many of us know what a pressure-cooker life has become, and no one is more vulnerable than a child who is already struggling. This may require that you sacrifice obligations and activities that seem essential to participate in, because sometimes you and your child need a free day to experience life without strict timetables.

For more tips on providing highly supportive homework help, see this book's website at http://www.newharbinger.com/40989. There, you'll find a step-by-step checklist for collaborating with your child on completing homework and other assignments.

Conclusion

If your child has ADHD, invariably he or she will have slowly emerging executive functioning skills. In order to meet the demands of studying, homework completion, time management, and keeping schoolwork organized, your child will need highly collaborative support from you. The amount of support you provide will vary and, at times, be quite significant. But I know of no other way to effectively help children with ADHD experience success at school and acquire executive functioning skills.

CHAPTER 11

Working with Your 11th or 12th Grader

Some children with LBLDs who successfully navigate elementary and middle school hit a wall when they enter the upper grades of high school. Content is more abstract and complex. Assignments are longer and more challenging. Quizzes and exams are more demanding. Even the hardest-working students can find themselves in over their heads. As your child navigates the final years of high school, the demands placed upon him or her will increase exponentially as the pace, volume, and complexity of the work increase in kind. Don't worry, though. With the strategies offered in this chapter—plus some hard work spent applying them—you and your child can overcome these challenges.

The story of Tim provides an excellent example of the difficulties a teen with LBLDs can encounter in eleventh and twelfth grades. For some of you, Tim's story may seem extreme. For others, Tim's story may precisely mirror the situations you have faced or are facing with your own child.

• Tim's Story

Several summers ago, Brenda, the mother of 17-year-old Tim, arranged a consultation with me. She shared that Tim was a bright young man who had struggled with LBLDs from a young age. As a child, Tim was good-natured and had a positive attitude. Unfortunately, Tim was beginning to struggle in a number of academic and personal life areas.

Brenda told me that Tim's slowly emerging written language skills and other executive functioning issues became significant problems once he entered high school. In ninth grade, Brenda arranged for Tim to get a 504 plan. With extra help from her, regular tutors, and his 504 plan accommodations, Tim was able to maintain a B average through tenth grade.

When Tim entered eleventh grade, the demands of school began to exceed his capacities. Suddenly, Tim was unable to keep up. Although he completed eleventh grade, passing most of his classes with C's and low B's, he had failed his Spanish 2 class.

Managing Upper-Grade Demands

Students with LBLDs frequently need more assistance in eleventh and twelfth grades than they did in the previous years. The extra help is needed to manage the increase in pace, volume, and complexity of the upper grades. Often the best way to move forward is to take a couple steps backward and offer even higher levels of support.

You might be thinking, "Shouldn't my teen be *more* independent now? Won't I be fostering a dependency on me that'll be hard to shake once my child graduates?" That I recommend a continued—and sometimes greater—level of support can come as a surprise. There is a fine line between being a helicopter parent and being a helpful parent. A helicopter parent provides help that is *not* needed, whereas a helpful parent provides help that *is* needed. By carefully analyzing your teen's needs and having an open and ongoing conversation with him or her, you will be able to determine what help is needed. By providing that help you are actually promoting independence, because a critical element of independence is knowing what help you need and how to get it.

In order for my collaborative approach of support to be successful with older children, you will need to adjust your mindset about when independence should be achieved. Teens often have rigid ideas about how they want things to be done and how much parents should be involved. By staying by your child's side and maintaining a healthy relationship, you are showing your child that you are confident that he or she will go off on his or her own once developmentally ready.

I also encourage you to become comfortable with the idea of *healthy dependence*. Healthy dependence is a manifestation of a successful attachment relationship in which a child recognizes his or her parents aren't going to abandon him or her in a moment of need. Being independent requires a number of higher-order skills. As we have learned, relative to their peers, teens with LBLDs need more time and support to acquire these skills. If a young adult does not exhibit independence, it generally means that he or she is simply not developmentally ready for it. I have seen many teens who struggled well into their twenties ultimately excel in their personal and professional lives. Until that happens, you and your child should both realize that dependence can be healthy and, in fact, a sign of a positive parent-child relationship.

Let's look at the three areas where school demands frequently exceed the capacities of eleventh- and twelfth-graders with LBLDs: pace, volume, and complexity. The strategies I offer here are the same that I used with Tim and his mom. They will help your family too.

Pace

In the upper grades, the frequency of tests, quizzes, and assignments dramatically increases. Additionally, a teacher's *delivery* (the number of words he or she says, the complexity of the words, and the lack of repetition) can often exceed the capabilities of a child with LBLDs. Furthermore, the demand to produce written or spoken language also increases. For instance, in the upper grades, teachers may expect a student who is called on to quickly organize his or her thoughts and provide a detailed response. It might be that a child with LBLDs is capable of such an answer; however, it's highly likely that more time will be needed to generate such a response.

Here's what you can do to support your child with the rigorous pace of upper grades:

- Frequently check the course website, or directly with your child's teacher, to evaluate the anticipated pace of instruction. Can your teen keep up? It is easy for a teen with an LBLD not to recognize that the fast pace is actually a challenge. Candidly discuss with your child that the pace is considerably quicker than in previous years. With this awareness, it is more likely that your teen will make an extra effort to be attentive in class and to plan ahead when it comes to project management.

- Create a weekly wall calendar. Indicate for each class not only important due dates and test dates but also start dates for assignments and test preparation. Include intermediate dates for completing portions of each assignment, along with the amount of preparation that should be accomplished for an upcoming test. This strategy will allow you and your child to manage the rapid pace at which important dates come up.

- Create a schedule of all daily activities. Working with your child, discuss strategies that will help him or her accomplish daily objectives.

- Have your teen generate a to-do list. Also include all the things he or she wants to do, such as extracurricalars and hobbies. Help him or her consider which of these priorities are urgent and which can be postponed. Discuss what desires might need to be put off until there is more time.

- Inevitably your child will miss something the teacher said in class, or an assignment will not be posted on the teacher's website. In these situations, you need to act fast if your child's grade has been affected. Have your child reach out to the teacher. See if your child can get an extension or if there's the possibility of doing an extra credit assignment to make up the missing work.

Volume

In the upper grades, there is a marked increase in the amount of reading, writing, and content. The increase in volume is often not proportional to the increase in a child's ability to handle the work. The assumption that the child should be able to complete this ever-increasing volume of work fails to take into account the child's LBLDs.

- Have a frank conversation with your teen about the increased volume. Help your teen compare the increased volume of work to what was expected of him or her only a year or two ago.

- Break the work into smaller, more manageable pieces. We often see decreased working memory capacities in children with LBLDs, which means they are less capable of simultaneously managing many different pieces of information. They are more likely to become overwhelmed and frustrated by a task. Take an active role in looking at the content your teen is required to learn and think about ways to break it into chunks.

Complexity

Complexity of schoolwork can mean ideas that are more abstract or information that is novel and unfamiliar. In upper grades, your child will start learning content for which he or she has little to no background information on which to draw. This will put him or her at an enormous disadvantage relative to his or her peers. For example, if your child is assigned to write an essay on the importance of the Supreme Court but has not learned about the three branches of the U.S. government, provide your child with a quick overview of the three branches and the role the Judicial Branch has as one of these branches. Even a brief over-view of background information can be enough to help your child manage the demands of the assignment.

- Encourage clarification from teachers. Because children with LBLDs benefit greatly from one-on-one interaction, advise your teen to seek out teachers to get clarification on challenging content.

- Encourage your teen to have patience. Help your teen under-stand that it is a characteristic, not a flaw, that he or she requires more time than classmates to learn certain things. Just because the rate at which your child processes information might be slower doesn't mean that ultimately the information won't get to where it needs to go. Helping a teen understand his or her learning process allows him or her to be more patient with him- or herself. Propose additional study time be built into the weekly routine to accommodate your teen's need for more review.

- Investigate additional school resources. Some teens are not aware of the extent to which their schools offer supplementary resources, such as videos, online support services, and other learning aids. You can look into whether these resources are available at your child's school and then gently guide your teen to utilize them.

By proactively helping your teen manage the increased pace, volume, and complexity of schoolwork in the upper grades, you will teach him or her essential skills that will ultimately allow for higher levels of independence.

The Importance of a Positive Mindset

Any time things are not going well for a teen, he or she will feel distressed and is likely to lapse into a state of negative thinking. If this happens to your child, it's likely you will begin to experience some of the stress and negative feelings as well. When I begin working with a family who is contending with a significant teen-related challenge, I encourage parents to focus on the things that are going well and leverage these thoughts into a positive mindset. This will encourage their teen to develop a more positive outlook as well.

Tim's Story (continued)

It was now midsummer, and Tim was supposed to start summer school to make up the Spanish 2 class he had failed. Tim told his mother that he was not going to summer school. A number of heated arguments between the two ensued.

In addition, Tim had just been fired from his summer job working in a skate shop. Tim loved skateboarding and had been excited about his first job. The firing came as a great blow to Tim, and he lapsed into a state of misery.

In the event your child is becoming discouraged by events in his or her life, you can help him or her develop an improved mindset by keeping things in perspective and finding a way to get comfortable with the things you cannot control. I know this is easier said than done. When your teen sees that you're comfortable with yourself and possess a sense of optimism, it will in turn help promote a positive mindset in him or her. Remind yourself and your teen that you are doing your best and that is all that can be expected of either one of you. The hard work you and your child invest in this process is well worth the effort. The results will have wide-reaching benefits for your teen and your relationship with him or her.

Dealing with Challenges

In the face of significant challenges and disappointments, allow yourself time to reflect on what is going on, and consider possible strategies to bring about improvement for your teen and yourself. Always keep in mind that time is a great healer and that your patience with a challenging situation is one of your best resources. Here are a few additional ideas on how to manage difficult situations:

- Recognize your child's feelings and talk about times in your own life when you have felt disappointment.

- De-escalate tension by communicating your ability to cope with whatever comes up.

- Help your teen maintain perspective; this experience will not define his or her entire life.

- Help your teen focus on the support he or she needs without comparing him- or herself to peers or siblings.

Tim's Story (continued)

To make matters worse, Tim was also having difficulty maintaining friendships. A girl he had been interested in had recently distanced herself from him. Tim's efforts to connect with his usual group of friends were also not working. Tim was confused, and his relationship with his mother was suffering. Tim was in a crisis, and so was Brenda.

As children transition into their junior and senior years of high school, their social groups often change. Their friendships become more complex and involve increasingly adult issues. It is often best for you to play the role of distant observer who is ready to offer advice when it is sought. If you are concerned about how your child is faring during this time, take a moment to observe any significant changes in his or her patterns in the following domains:

- Mood

- Health

- Personal grooming

- Weight gain or loss

- Wardrobe

- Daily schedule

- Social patterns

- School performance

In the event you detect unusual changes in these areas, it might be good to consider a gentle conversation with your child. Keep the talk respectful by phrasing questions in an open-ended way. For example, "How are things going for you?" If your efforts are met with resistance, you may want to consider a consultation with a mental health professional for more specific guidance with regard to your concerns.

Tim's Story (continued)

I suggested to Brenda that Tim meet with me. Several days later, Brenda called back to explain that Tim refused to come in. I suggested that she tell him that meeting with me was simply to start making a plan for how Tim might be able to pursue his dream of attending a four-year college. This strategy worked.

Several days later, Tim arrived at my office. I was met by a tall, thin young man with straight brown hair that hung over his shoulders. Everything about Tim's posture, demeanor, and even handshake suggested that he was deeply demoralized. Tim shared with me that it had always been his ambition to work in sports journalism. My encouragement was met with a huge measure of defeat on Tim's part. "I'll never be able to be a sports writer," Tim said. "I've really screwed my life up."

It had always been Tim's plan to attend a four-year college, but this plan was beginning to appear difficult to achieve. When I asked Tim about his upcoming summer Spanish class, he seemed utterly defeated. Tim told me that he was not going to take the class because he no longer felt that college was a realistic possibility for him. Tim went on to tell me that his plan was to drop out of high school and take the GED.

Tim shared with me how disappointed he was about losing his job at the skate shop. I learned that Tim had been staying up late playing video games, which made it difficult for him to be up in time for his job in the morning. Evidently, Tim's frequent tardiness had become too much for his employer. After several warnings, Tim was fired.

Before things were going to get better for Tim, he needed to feel better about himself and his prospects.

Keys to Boosting a Teen's Morale

We all know that a confident leader instills confidence in those around him or her. Your confidence will become your teen's confidence. Lead by example. Stay comfortable in your own skin. Try to be as positive as possible, even if the circumstances are challenging. Here are ways to do this:

- Double down on your optimism for your child and your belief in him or her as a wonderful, worthy person.

- Provide your teen with explicit examples of his or her worth. Share the nice things people have said about him or her.

- Avoid the hobgoblin of tough love. Sink-or-swim approaches rarely have positive outcomes.

- Be cautious with constructive criticism. Constructive criticism is still criticism. By the time a teen with LBLDs has gotten to a point of low morale, he or she has had enough criticism.

- Remind your teen that school is not the only source of identity or validation. Help your teen follow his or her interests outside of school. Skills developed off campus will still benefit him or her in school.

Tim's Story (continued)

I began providing Tim with a significant amount of support. First, we worked on a strategy to get back his job at the skate shop. Tim and I crafted a well-written letter apologizing for his tardiness and explaining why it had occurred. The letter also detailed how he intended to change his lifestyle to manage his job responsibilities.

Tim was rewarded several days later with a reply from the shop stating that they would allow him to resume as long as he's always on time for work. With this new incentive to get sufficient sleep, Tim determined how long he would allow himself to play video games and what time he needed to go to bed. Tim was surprised to learn how healthy he felt after getting several nights of sufficient sleep. Until this point, he did not believe his lack of sleep was impacting his ability to function during the day.

As Tim began to regain his self-esteem, we started to turn our attention toward his career goal of sports writing and a path he might take to get there. We reviewed requirements for some of the colleges Tim thought he would like to attend. Tim would need to have completed two years of a foreign language in high school. With the added incentive of attending a college that appealed to him, Tim shifted his thinking and decided to take the Spanish 2 summer school class. He ended up earning a respectable grade.

As the fall approached, we discovered Tim's school offered an alternative English class that would allow him to submit sports blogs for credit. Tim began to recognize that he had an opportunity to be a successful student in his senior year if he continued to accept help.

Tips for Providing Academic Assistance to Teens

Teens with LBLDs frequently need a high level of academic assistance. However, even in the best of circumstances, it is difficult for teens to accept help even when they need it. This difficulty stems from their observation that many of their peers seem to navigate school and life successfully with a high level of independence. As a parent of a child with an LBLD you can normalize your teen's need for help by taking into account the strategies here:

- Discuss how common it is to get help. Assure your teen that getting help now won't render him or her dependent for the rest of his or her life.

- Teach the value of asking for help, and teach how to accept help without shame. Demonstrate the value of getting help by getting help together. Asking a counselor or resource specialist for assistance shows your teen that seeking help is nothing to be ashamed of.

- Help your teen understand that there are many reasons one individual is different from another; those differences necessitate different types of support.

- Emphasize that your support is a collaboration of equals. Solve problems together.

- Model how you would manage a task. Imagine you are the one who has to contend with the demand. What would you do? Offer your thought process.

- Empathize with your teen about the challenges he or she is facing. Share your thoughts about why an assignment, course load, or teaching method is challenging.

Tim's Story (continued)

During the remainder of the summer, Tim exhibited higher levels of maturity at work, and he was able to continue to work part-time during the school year. This experience gave him a sense of responsibility. Additionally, through his frequent interaction with customers, Tim developed a number of positive social skills. Tim also made a new group of friends, which further decreased the time he spent playing video games.

Tim began to develop a more positive attitude about himself and school. Although Tim required the support of a tutor and some additional accommodations through his 504 plan, he graduated from high school and enrolled in a community college.

After successfully completing community college, Tim was able to transfer to a four-year college with a strong communications program. Tim is currently completing college and enjoying considerable success in many facets of his life. He still lives at home, but he and Brenda are both following a plan to increase Tim's independence incrementally each semester. Brenda has now grown comfortable with where Tim is, and their relationship is strong again.

Conclusion

Supporting your teen through eleventh and twelfth grades will require significant adjustments. Teens undergo many developmental changes during this time and are beginning to identify themselves as adults. You can leverage this by recognizing their maturity and ability to manage some responsibilities with greater levels of independence. But it is important not to lose sight of the fact that even though many teens in the upper grades are capable of high levels of independence, teens with LBLDs frequently need ongoing help to manage the increased demands of school and life. Your teen may continue to need your support in the areas of organization, time management, and self-advocacy, in addition to needing help with the surge in reading and writing assignments. Providing your teen with the support he or she needs in the upper grades is one of the best ways to help him or her finish high school on a strong note and begin a successful transition to the next phase of life.

Part III

Succeeding
at Life

CHAPTER 12

Navigating Life
Outside of School

Although most of this book is about helping your child learn as much in school as possible, parents also ask me how they can support their child in various day-to-day scenarios. The challenges children with language-based learning difficulties experience affect them on campus and off in direct and indirect ways. Remember that at school, your child has a steady stream of adults who can help him or her navigate the day. Outside of school, however, your child relies almost solely on you for guidance. This is good, because as a parent, you are your child's best resource for helping him or her deal with complex life challenges.

This chapter offers strategies for promoting social skills, managing anxiety, developing a healthy lifestyle, promoting financial responsibility, and making the most of your child's summer vacations. Although this list isn't exhaustive, these are some of the common issues that arise in my practice.

Promoting Social Skills

While most children have frequent opportunities to socialize outside of school, many children with LBLDs have fewer opportunities. Slowly emerging speaking and listening skills often impede communication. As children grow older, they are more likely to recognize that they are different, resulting in increased anxiety about social interactions. Martha Denckla explains that LBLDs are a social skills disability (Denckla 2013), and in addition, that children with LBLDs are more likely to experience feelings of social isolation (Lavoie 2007). Helping your child make friends can sometimes take what seems to be a circuitous route.

Teach Your Child Communication Skills

While at school, most children are familiar with one another, have a set of shared experiences, and rely on the existing social structure to facilitate child-to-child interactions. Outside of school, however, such interactions can be challenging for some children with LBLDs. It is not uncommon for these children to have difficulty reading social cues or engaging in productive conversations.

Moreover, many children are not always able to determine when a peer with a language-based learning difficulty is challenged by a conversation or has lost track of the topic at hand. This can result in the child with the LBLD feeling left out or confused, or responding inappropriately.

You can help your child develop the social and language skills he or she needs to communicate effectively with peers by frequently modeling and practicing good communication. All of this will translate into improved oral expression, listening comprehension, social skills development, and learning. As a parent, you probably already model good manners using words such as "please" and "thank you" without much thought. You can also model good communication practices for conversation in general. Try the following strategies throughout your day together, and eventually your child will become more skilled at conversing and making meaningful connections with others.

Create opportunities to have conversations. With electronics, social media, and other distractions, you have a lot of competition. Make conversation time with your child electronics free. Meals and commutes are perfect times to work on your child's communication skills. Increase your odds of effective conversation by taking walks, engaging in arts and crafts projects, playing board games, doing chores around the house, and going to the store together.

Don't force conversations. If your child does not seem to be in a communicative mood, don't force it. Just being together, even without conversation—and still without electronics—will help your child learn that you accept him or her completely. Likewise, if you are talking and you recognize that his or her frustration threshold is approaching, switch tactics, which may mean ending the conversation. As a general rule, pushing a child to communicate when he or she is not up to it ends up being counterproductive.

Choose topics that are interesting to your child. Keep your interests at bay if your child doesn't share them. You might start out: "What did you enjoy about _____ [the movie, school today, etc.]?" or "Tell me something fun about what you did _____ [at school, in the yard, etc.]."

Let your child guide the conversation. When you allow your son or daughter to set the topic of the conversation, you're making it clear that you're interested in what she or he has to say. Some children with LBLDs rarely get to lead a discussion. When your child is with you, it's his or her chance to lead. Be the listener.

Speak at his or her level. Choose words that you know your child will understand, and speak at a rate that you know your child will keep up with. Sometimes it is helpful to slow down the rate at which we speak and to restate the same idea several times in slightly different ways. Read your child's facial expression to determine if he or she understands what it is you are trying to communicate.

Allow your child "thinking time." This way, he or she does not feel pressured to respond. Your child will talk when ready and do so from a calm state.

Keep your child talking. One way to do this is to encourage his or her line of reasoning, even if you don't agree with it. If you are not sure what your child is trying to express, you can, after a period of time, ask for help: "Please help me understand what your feelings/thoughts are." You can also restate what your child has said to check for understanding: "So, if I understand you correctly, you have a plan to improve the environment by encouraging people to plant trees that also bear edible fruit. Is that what you're trying to say?"

Offer your child positive reinforcement. Children aren't used to feeling valued as conversationalists. So provide encouraging feedback when appropriate, such as when he or she shares an observation on his or her own. You could say, "You said that very well." Another way to provide positive reinforcement is around others. When your child is within earshot, share with someone (your partner, a friend, a teacher) that your child is an excellent conversationalist. Let that person know what your child was talking about and how much you enjoyed the conversation.

Take advantage of teachable moments. A further benefit of frequently practicing communication with your child is that, when your child responds inappropriately, you can guide him or her to a more appropriate response and reinforce a positive learning outcome. If your child said, "I hate all the kids in my classroom," you might want to respond by saying, "Several of the kids in your classroom are your friends and they like you very much. Are you sure you hate all the kids in your classroom?"

Help Ease Social Anxiety

It is not unusual for children with LBLDs to experience high levels of anxiety in social situations. This anxiety can lead to social withdrawal, antisocial behavior, or disruptive behavior. In addition, social anxiety can inhibit or limit a child's ability to express his or her thoughts. These children might initiate topics of conversation that are inappropriate, speak more than necessary, speak too loudly, or use unsuitable language.

Social anxiety can also be expressed in types of physical behavior that are inappropriate, such as grabbing, pushing, squeezing, and rough-housing. At times, these actions can take on a significant degree of intensity. While some level of grabbing and pushing is customary for young children, as they get older, this type of behavior can be viewed as highly inappropriate, especially in the teen years. Whereas many teens begin to naturally make the switch to more adult interactions, some teens with LBLDs might not fully appreciate how the social dynamics around them are changing. This disconnect can lead to diminished friendships or social isolation.

To promote better communication and social skills, try these strategies:

Regularly observe your child's social interactions. When you observe verbal interaction that appears inappropriate, be strategic in how you address the matter with your child. Try to avoid any level of public humiliation.

Discuss what you observed. Choose a good time to have a gentle conversation with your child about what happened. Begin the conversation by complimenting the fact that your child is wonderful and much liked by his or her friends. Point out good qualities and characteristics that your son or daughter has. Then ask your child how he or she feels a particular situation is going. Almost always, a child will recognize when he or she has gone a little overboard.

Give feedback. If your son or daughter is forthcoming about his or her actions, compliment your child on being truthful. If your child is unable to identify what he or she has done wrong, gently point out that the other children are taking turns when it comes to talking, or that his or her roughhousing seems to be more intense than the other children want.

Teach Your Child How to Join Conversations

Children with LBLDs often have difficulty determining the best way to interact with other children. The more often your child is able to engage in a productive social interaction, the more likely it is that he or she will choose to engage in future social interactions.

Teach your child to observe social interactions before joining them. Practice this skill by watching and then discussing social interactions around you or on TV. Many reality TV shows provide opportunities to observe individuals with a wide range of socials skills—the good, the bad, and the ugly. Share your observations with your child. Discuss the strengths of the good interactions you observe, and share ideas about how the bad or ugly interactions could have been improved.

Ask your child to think of ways to join a conversation. Share with your child a three-step method for entering a conversation:

1. Listen carefully to the conversation until you have a good idea of what the topic is.

2. Think of a related idea to introduce to the conversation.

3. Wait for a lull in the conversation and then introduce your idea.

Show appreciation for listening. If your child is reluctant to speak while in a group, that is okay. Remind your child that taking the role of thoughtful listener is one of the best ways to signal to others that you are good company. Other children will notice that your child is listening and therefore is an active participant in the conversation.

Help Your Child Join a Group or Sports Team

Organized groups such as the Boy Scouts, Girl Scouts, religious youth groups, science clubs, and sports teams are good places for your child to develop social skills. Your child is more likely to develop a friendship when it begins with a shared interest. Here are a few strategies you can use to help your child join a group successfully:

Make sure your child wants to join the group. Your child will be more motivated to participate if he or she has an authentic interest in the group. Spend some time on the Internet exploring different groups and see if there is something that catches your child's attention. Your child can also attend a couple of youth sport events or try a sample class to help determine what group, class, or team he or she would like to join. Your child might even consider starting his or her own group.

Learn about the group ahead of time. Before your child attends the first meeting or practice, help him or her learn as much as possible about the group and its members. Check the group's website; observe a meeting, class, or practice; and talk to the group leader and other parents who have children in the group. Reach out to the group leader to see if your child can meet someone already in the group before attending the first meeting. If your child is nervous, remind him or her that it's okay and that it takes a while to develop the knowledge base that the other members might have. You might say, "A lot of the other kids have been involved in this for a long time. You are new to this so you are not expected to be an expert, but one day you will be."

Encourage building a friendship. Once your child starts participating in a group, encourage your son or daughter to meet with one or two members outside of the group, so that he or she can strengthen some friendships within it. You might start by speaking with other parents in the group to help facilitate this, but it really depends on your child and what will help him or her feel most comfortable. Some children are easily embarrassed by any parent involvement. Other children don't mind.

Jump-Start Social Activities for Your Child

Children with LBLDs frequently benefit from support in engaging in positive social activities. Here are some tips for organizing playdates and groups outings, as well as for communicating with parents and other adults who might be supervising your child during a social event.

Tips for Organizing Successful Playdates, Sleepovers, and Group Outings

In terms of building social skills, the quality of each interaction is more important than the quantity of interactions. When your child has the chance to have a playdate, attend a sleepover, or go out with friends, the best way to help him or her is to invest a little effort in making sure the interaction goes as well as it can.

- Carefully time playdates. It's okay if playdates are short, between one and two hours. Avoid scheduling a playdate when you know your child is likely to be tired or hungry. For some children, this means right after school, a common playdate time. Bring to the playdate what you know your child will need, such as snacks for everyone if you believe your child will get hungry or a craft activity everyone can do if you know your child is too tired to run around.

- Don't force your child into activities he or she may not enjoy, and don't force him or her to go places that cause anxiety. It can be tempting to bring your child where you know other children will be, such as an ice cream store, playground, or park. But if your child already tends to withdraw socially in these places, he or she will retreat even further in these settings.

- Assess the complexity of board games. Children with LBLDs may be challenged by board games with complicated rules. Before introducing a board game in front of friends and siblings, make sure your child has had a chance to practice and learn the game at his or her own pace. Make an effort to keep on hand the types of games and activities that are popular in your child's social circle, and give your child the chance to practice them if he or she is interested.

- Wait to schedule a sleepover for your child until he or she asks for one. Children are ready to spend the night at a friend's house at different times. It's not an activity you should force, no matter how tempting it might be. If your child isn't ready to spend the night out but has been invited to a sleepover, use the opportunity to show your child that you are a reliable source of support and will not reveal your child's discomfort. Tell your child that you will explain to the host that you already have a plan for the next day and that your child needs to be home by a certain time to get enough rest.

- Plan a faux-sleepover. At your house or at a friend's, children can have dinner, put on pajamas, watch a movie, and then get picked up right before bedtime. Even older children can use this routine if they are not yet comfortable spending the night away from home.

- Help your child feel safe while on a group outing. Once you and your child are ready for a group outing, it's important to invest a little extra effort to practice logistics, such as what to do if he or she is lost or if an emergency arises; where he or she should wait for pickup; and how often your child should check in with you. Make sure that any directions are exact and that your child has the chance to practice going to the pickup spot you've identified. You can help your child set alerts on his or her phone at times when he or she should check in with you. Also, make sure your child knows the information he or she should tell you when you do connect by phone.

Children with LBLDs may need extra support and practice in these areas to be comfortable and competent in keeping themselves safe while out with their friends. That's okay. You will know when your child is fully ready, but if you are unsure, share your feelings with your child and encourage him or her to do the same.

Tips for Talking to Other Parents

Most parents naturally gravitate toward families with similar parenting styles. This makes communicating with other parents easier, but there are still a few points to keep in mind when trying to structure positive social interactions for children with LBLDs:

- Before sending your child to a friend's home for the first time, ask the parents about their house rules and how they prefer to be addressed. Review these with your child and practice.

- It can be hard to accurately predict how long a playdate should last to be considered a success. Children who have slowly emerging social skills may expend their capacity for self-control sooner than their peers. You will help your child by ending playdates before your child reaches that point. Trust your instincts about how long a playdate should be, and check in with the host family midway. You may need to pick up your child earlier, or your child may be able to play longer than you originally thought.

- Parents who are hosting your child will benefit from your reassurance that they can contact you at any time during a playdate. Stay flexible and available in the event your input is needed.

Tips for Talking with Youth Group Leaders and Coaches

Like your child's schoolteachers, group leaders and sport coaches provide instruction to your child. Communicate with these adults in the same respectful manner you approach your child's teachers.

- Request a brief ten- to fifteen-minute meeting with the adult in charge when your child first joins a group.

- At the initial meeting, let the leader or coach know that your child has LBLDs. Explain how those challenges may impact his or her participation or ability to follow directions.

- Provide a brief profile of your child's learning characteristics and how he or she seems to learn best.

- Make sure these adults know they can contact you at any time regarding your child.

- If the demands of the activity exceed your child's capacities, determine if the activity or the instructional style can be modified to better suit your child. Meet again with your child's leader or coach. If the situation cannot be easily modified, there may be a similar group or league that is a better match for your child's capacities.

- Remember that extracurricular activities should be a source of fun for your child. If the activity isn't fun, reconsider your child's participation.

Monitor Social Media and Technology

As a parent, you control how old your child must be to access and possess a variety of technological tools. Helping your child with LBLDs navigate the technology landscape will require additional supervision and support, because slowly emerging capacities for reading, writing, and attention will affect your child's ability to use technology.

First, establish house rules for when and how your child accesses technological devices. Then set up a way to monitor your child's use across all devices. Work together as a family to determine the best way to do this. Incorporating your child's input on boundaries is a good way to collaborate, and children often have pretty good ideas about what is fair and reasonable.

Next, ask your child about his or her goals for social media. Is it to connect and communicate with specific friends? Participate in a large group? Stay informed of current trends? Discuss how the method he or she is choosing meets or doesn't meet these goals. Keep in mind that it's easy for children to follow a group of peers without considering the consequences of their actions. If your child's LBLDs increase the likelihood that he or she will act impulsively, you'll need to help your child develop thoughtfulness about his or her use of technology, especially when communicating on social media and other platforms.

Talk with your child about the advantages and the dangers of the technology he or she is using. What does your child already know? What has your child not been made aware of yet? Be sure to discuss cyberbullying. Using current events as examples, talk about how posts and comments affect others. Encourage your child to share feelings about the comments he or she sees to develop an awareness of cyberbullying. Discuss the consequences of inappropriate postings, such as rejection from colleges. Discuss types of postings that are illegal. Don't assume your child already knows this information from school or friends.

Managing Anxiety and Stress

In small doses, stress is good. It helps us stay focused and remember the important things we learn. The downside is that chronically elevated levels of cortisol, the hormone released when we are stressed, are destructive to not only the brain but also the body. The regions of the brain that are especially affected are those dedicated to learning and memory, such as the prefrontal cortex and hippocampus.

Children with LBLDs experience plenty of stress trying to keep up at school. As a parent, you can help your child respond to stress using these strategies:

- Determine when your child is experiencing stress. He or she may seem short-tempered, withdrawn, distracted, or antsy. Disruptive behavior is also a sign of stress.

- Take corrective action. Help your child stop what he or she is doing and engage in another activity that is not as stressful.

- Encourage vigorous physical activity. Exercise is an excellent means of dissipating cortisol buildup. If your child is experiencing chronically high stress, take frequent breaks during homework. Easy exercise options to try in short intervals are jumping rope, sit-ups, push-ups, yoga poses like plank or downward-facing dog, basketball (free-throw practice), and catch (baseball, Frisbee, lacrosse, etc.).

- Start talking. Sometimes just engaging your child in a conversation about an interesting topic can significantly reduce his or her stress.

- Lead your child (or use an app or online resource) to engage in a short meditative or mindfulness exercise. Find a quiet, comfortable place for your child to sit. Have your child settle into a comfortable position, close his or her eyes, and take a few slow deep breaths. Talk your child and yourself through these steps: clear your mind by actively "pushing out" as many thoughts as you can. Imagine something calming, such as a leaf gently floating toward the ground. Hang on to the calming thought for as long as possible, and focus only on slow, deep breathing and the calming thought. At the outset, it may only be possible to meditate in this way for sixty seconds or so. But over time, the length of the meditation will extend. If staying still in this way further agitates your child, move on quickly to another strategy. There is no benefit to making these attempts more stressful.

- Engage in a fun activity for a few minutes. Take a few turns at a board game or a puzzle. Take a few minutes to look up at the clouds or play with a family pet.

- Do something to help someone else, or fix something that's broken. The opportunity to be helpful can boost confidence when tasks seem overwhelming.

Developing a Healthy Lifestyle

Because children tend to be healthy and energetic, it is easy for them to not appreciate the importance of getting enough rest, eating healthy food, and engaging in regular exercise. Optimal brain development, however, requires a healthy balance of all three. Let's look at some strategies I've used with a variety of children to help them develop healthy habits.

Sleep

Nothing is more essential for a healthy and well-functioning brain than sleep. Indeed, many stress-related issues can be reduced with healthy sleep habits (Fuligni and Hardway 2006). In addition, students who make a point of getting adequate sleep get better grades (Hershner and Chervin 2014). We know that fatigue significantly inhibits learning capacities, yet that knowledge rarely makes an impression on young people.

I find it useful to teach my students that their brain occupies only 3 percent of their body mass but uses approximately 25 percent of their caloric intake. In other words, their brains are working really hard all of the time! I tell them that sleep is when our brains rest and process what they've learned during the course of the day. I also explain that sleep is when our brains have an opportunity to discharge a build-up of harmful chemicals and byproducts. Without sleep, our brains do not discharge these harmful substances.

Help your child get as much exercise as possible during the day. Help him or her complete as many necessary tasks (homework, chores, other responsibilities) as possible so that nothing is hanging over his or her head at bedtime.

Help your child go to sleep and wake up at the same time every day. Try to keep as close as possible to this schedule, even on the weekends. About an hour before bedtime, put the house to sleep. Turn off as many lights as possible. Turn off as many electrical devices as possible. Most people sleep best in cool, dark rooms, with a small amount of white noise from a fan or white-noise maker. You may want to try this in your child's room.

Nutrition

Teaching kids about good nutrition is a whole lot easier today with gardens in schools, the farm-to-table movement, and the celebrity status of chefs. Cooking is rapidly becoming a profession of choice for many youngsters. You can take advantage of this wonderful new trend by watching cooking shows with your child and cooking together. With your child, find engaging videos to watch on cooking and nutrition. You can also research healthy recipes on the Internet together and encourage your child to begin his or her own collection of recipes.

Help your child understand the underlying reasons a healthy diet is beneficial. Then, allow your child to create a menu for the week. Take your child with you while shopping for the required ingredients. Then, encourage your child to assist you in the preparation of these meals.

Finally, you can help your child join cooking-based interest groups online and in person.

Exercise

In addition to promoting growth and development, physical activity also promotes learning and memory (Neighmond 2006). Furthermore, physical activity is known to be a protective factor against many types of illnesses and a number of the common psychiatric issues faced by some teens, such as depression and anxiety (Hershner and Chervin 2014).

With your child, find engaging videos to watch on the value of exercise. Help your child understand the underlying reasons exercise is beneficial to the body and mind. Allow your child to create a weekly exercise regimen. Encourage him or her to invite friends to be part of these exercise activities.

Help your child maintain the schedule he or she has made. On the days when your child would rather stay home and play video games, redirect him or her to the exercise routine you've established: Remind your son or daughter of the great job he or she is doing. Help him or her remember how good it feels when exercising is finished. You can also create an extra incentive to exercise by taking your child somewhere new, like an indoor rock wall or an ice skating rink.

Promoting Financial Responsibility

Children with LBLDs frequently struggle with numeracy, sequencing, and attention to detail. These characteristics make receiving an early introduction to financial responsibilities especially important. As with virtually all of the strategies provided in this book, teaching your child financial responsibility will require additional levels of modeling and support from you.

When you feel that your child is ready, set aside time to speak with him or her about the importance of money management. There are children's books about money management for all ages and reading levels. Read one of these books together as a conversation starter about how your child would like to spend or save money that he or she earns. Encouraging a child to save money for a special item or charitable donation is a way parents can begin instruction on this topic. You can open a bank account while your child is still living at home so you can collaboratively balance his or her account and discuss whether his or her spending and saving are furthering his or her goals. An incremental process for earning and saving money helps children learn planning and patience.

As your child matures, work with him or her to create a budget to manage personal expenses. Help your child understand what steps are needed to stay within that budget. New financial planning programs and apps are introduced frequently. Evaluate a few that seem suitable for your child's needs and put them on appropriate devices.

Young adults also need to learn how to use credit and debit cards responsibly. Additionally, although most account balancing is now done online, learning to do these tasks on paper may be a more effective way to teach children with LBLDs these fundamental skills.

Making the Most of Summer Vacation

During the summer, you have the chance to let your child engage in something he or she likes to do and is good at—to experience excelling rather than struggling. I firmly believe that experiences of success are better at promoting brain development than any schoolwork your child might do during the school year. Children really need this time to decompress. I am a big believer in making unstructured activities a priority, because I am a big believer in balance.

School is so structured and the need to get homework done is so important that there aren't many hours in the day for children (or parents) to have downtime. Unstructured activities are those that allow for exploration to play, to choose what to do, and to choose the people with whom they spend time. These activities can be as simple as watching movies at home, playing at recess, or walking around the neighborhood. If you have a child who likes physical activities, seek out parks and recreation centers. If you have an artist, keep a roll of craft paper handy and let your child paint or draw in large scale without aiming for a specific result.

Remember that summer is a vacation for you too. Just as your child should be able to choose enjoyable activities, you should also be able to choose pursuits that will help you refresh and recharge.

Summer jobs and volunteer opportunities may not be easy for minors to come by. Your child will likely need your help to research available positions. Once you have identified where the opportunities may be, help your child request an application. Your child may also need your help to complete the form and draft a résumé. Make sure to keep the answers in your child's words and accurately reflect his or her abilities.

Learning Enrichment in the Summer?

Sometimes it can be helpful to set aside time for academic work, as long as your child responds to it in a positive way. However, forcing a child to do something that results in high levels of stress and disrupts the quality of your relationship with him or her is likely to do more harm than good. If this is the case in your home, wait until a few weeks before school resumes to tackle academic work.

You'll want to get some "buy-in" from your child before starting. All children like the feeling of being successful in class. Your child will be encouraged to work with you if he or she understands that the summertime work will help him or her feel successful during the first weeks of school.

There is a tendency to want to review the previous year's school material, especially if your child struggled. Although there is logic to this approach, it is not as effective as pre-teaching upcoming school material—one of the best ways to help prepare a child for a successful school year. So before summer begins, arrange a meeting with a school official to see if textbooks and other materials your child will receive in the fall can be provided early. If possible, meet with your child's future teachers to learn what topics will be taught in the first two months of school.

Create a study plan with the input of your child. Decide what days and times you will work together. Generally, three to four days a week can be adequate. (If you would like to allocate more time, consider working two or three days a week throughout the entire summer.) Then create a manageable schedule and routine for each session. A common strategy is to do about ten minutes of instruction for each grade level. If your child is entering first grade, ten minutes should be sufficient per session. If your child is entering second grade, twenty minutes should be sufficient, and so on.

While pre-teaching, express your own curiosity about what your son or daughter will be learning. Your curiosity will inspire your child's curiosity. When a child starts the new school year with an understanding of the content ahead, he or she is much more likely to understand class lectures, manage the demands of assignments, and succeed in school.

The strategies offered here will only work if you are able to implement them calmly. It's a tall order, I know. But I also know that when we respond to a child who is dysregulated in a manner that is also dysregulated, we prolong or escalate whatever the problem might be. When we respond to a child with a sense of calm and wait until our message can be heard and applied, resolution happens. An excellent example of this approach in action is the story of Nancy and her son, Alec, who struggled with LBLDs.

• Alec's Story

It was late summer, and the new school year was approaching fast. Nancy had a plan to complete several summer reading and writing assignments with her son, Alec. She decided that today was the day to start on the assignments. Alec was a pleasant and spirited eighth-grader, but the idea of doing schoolwork did not appeal to him on this warm summer afternoon.

Alec had a different plan. He was going to hop on his bike and ride over to his friend's house to play video games. A lively argument between mother and son ensued. Neither would budge. It was a stalemate.

Then Nancy had an idea. She went into the kitchen and exclaimed, "Oh, darn! Why won't this window open? Alec, can you help me figure out what's wrong with this window?"

"No," Alec replied. He was feeling glum. The school year was getting closer with each passing day.

Nancy thought quickly. "It's so hot in here. I sure wish I could get some fresh air." Then she waited.

Her patience was rewarded. From the other room, Nancy heard Alec mumble, "I know what the problem is."

"You do?" Nancy gently asked.

Alec knew their windows had recently been painted. He grabbed a screwdriver and dashed out the door. Moments later, he was able to nudge the window open.

"Wow! Alec, thanks so much! How did you know what to do?" Nancy inquired.

"I watched them paint it and I saw the paint dripping down. I knew it would get stuck," Alec answered. "Do you want me to fix the other windows?"

"That would be great! Thanks so much for helping out," Nancy said.

Half an hour later, Alec proudly returned from his chore. He was beaming with pride. Nancy knew a good thing when she saw it. "Alec, you are such a great helper. I bet you could fix a bunch of other things if you had a few more tools. What do you say we jump in the car and drive to the hardware store so you can pick out some tools?"

"Really, Mom?!" Alec was excited by this prospect. He felt appreciated for what he could do and liked being recognized for his abilities.

Alec and Nancy had a terrific afternoon. After a successful trip to the hardware store, they stopped for burgers and fries. All afternoon, Alec talked about the many things he was going to fix around the house. As they drove home, Nancy gently said, "I bet we could get through a lot of your summer assignments quickly if we work together. What do you say we take a quick look at them and then decide if it's something we want to do?"

Alec was quiet. Nancy went on, "If we decide it's just too much, we won't do it, and that will be okay with me. What do you say?"

"Okay, Mom," Alec said.

When they got home, Nancy found a way to get Alec involved. Within an hour, they had completed a lot of the reading and writing, and Alec and Nancy felt great.

Although Nancy's proposal to work on summer assignments was met with resistance, she was able to redirect Alec toward an activity that she knew would result in a positive outcome. Her plan worked, albeit with a bit of theater on her part. A bit of drama, even when its contrivance is detected by a teen, can still work. There's an unwritten rule among children and teens: if an adult has good intentions, a teen will tolerate a certain amount of scheming. Never underestimate this rule when navigating challenging waters!

Nancy listened carefully to the tone of Alec's refusal. She knew he was feeling glum. Nancy used her insight to stay attuned, which informed her subsequent decisions. She knew that getting him to do something that he was capable of doing well would get him out of his bad mood and ready—eventually—to learn. Ultimately, he had success with the windows and was proud of himself. He had accomplished something, which always feels good, especially to a child with LBLDs, for whom so many things go wrong.

Nancy knew to build on success. She offered to take Alec to the hardware store to buy some tools so he could fix other things around the house. This was not a planned reward, and it was motivated by an internal process. The *process* was being rewarded. This is very different from a conditional reward, a this-for-that perk. Nancy's reward instead said, "Wow, the direction we are going is good. Let's keep it going!"

Having positive experiences with your child strengthens your relationship. Alec's shift into a positive mindset and his enjoyment of being with his mom diminished his resistance to working on the summer assignment. Nancy and Alec were able to work together to complete it.

If you speed through those good times, you can lose some of what was just gained. When something is going well, keep it going. Honor the moment and let it last. You will get the most out of it that way.

Conclusion

For children with language-based learning difficulties, many of the challenges they experience at school are also felt outside of it. As a parent, you can create opportunities to balance your child's schedule so that he or she experiences optimal amounts of structured and unstructured time. You can help promote social skills, and you can lessen your child's anxiety by structuring activities that will enhance the quality of his or her experiences. Additionally, you can help your child boost specific academic skills to ease his or her transition into the coming school year.

By systematically implementing the strategies suggested in this chapter, your son or daughter can build skills that will help him or her not only be more successful outside of school but also while at school and beyond. In the next chapter, I will describe how many of the strategies addressed here are modified to promote success for young adults as they transition into adulthood.

CHAPTER 13

Cultivating Independence After High School*

As teens transition into adulthood, they face complex challenges that we often expect them to handle on their own. But even well-equipped teens can have trouble fulfilling responsibilities, navigating relationships, exercising good judgment, and charting a course to a happy future. Teens with language-based learning difficulties tend to experience more difficulty in these areas.

In chapter 1, we discussed the Matthew Effect, whereby reading skills improve faster in good readers than they do in poor readers because good readers read more. This effect can also be seen in the development of life skills. Because teens with LBLDs have less practice handling things on their own, they are less likely to be self-sufficient when we might expect them to be. This disadvantage means that they may not be ready to practice life skills until they're older.

This delay may cause discomfort. You may feel the pressure of your community's expectation for your teen to be more independent, along with societal blame placed on parents or the teen for these delays. However, much of our society has lost sight of the fact that teens with LBLDs are experiencing escalating life challenges at precisely the same time they are being told they should *not* be seeking or receiving high levels of support.

---

* This chapter was written in collaboration with Crystal I. Lee.

How do we promote independence in teens and young adults? It is not an exact science. In fact, the prefrontal cortex, which is required to achieve high levels of independence, is often not fully developed until people are in their late twenties or even older. Instead of thinking of adolescents as directly transitioning into adulthood, Jeffrey Jensen Arnett, a leading expert on young adults, suggests that they enter a new developmental phase he terms "emerging adulthood" (Arnett 2014). This developmental period spans the ages eighteen to twenty-nine. Arnett's paradigm takes into account that the transition to adulthood is often slow and complex. During this time, emerging adults face immense societal pressure to establish their identities, build adult relationships, and find fulfilling career paths. This is a lot to ask of any emerging adult, especially one with a language-based learning difficulty. A negative feedback loop develops when an emerging adult encounters frequent difficulty in the absence of appropriate support, making bad situations worse. To prevent this, we recommend high levels of ongoing support.

Academic Options After High School

In order for emerging adults to successfully navigate the world and compete for jobs, it is essential that they have enough time to develop their written language and executive functioning skills. We believe for some students the best way to accomplish this is *continuing* formal education after high school.

Higher education programs provide structured, supportive environments in which emerging adults, particularly those with LBLDs, can continue to practice and develop skills as they mature. In addition to developing academic and executive functioning skills, higher education programs allow emerging adults the chance to manage bureaucratic demands such as completing applications, paying fees, securing living quarters, and enrolling in classes.

Finding the Appropriate College

There are many options for education after high school. We recommend carefully considering your child's strengths and needs. In addition to four-year colleges, investigate a variety of options such as vocational programs, community colleges, and programs designed for students with learning differences. You can expand your search even further to include online courses, part-time courses, and individualized coaching or instruction.

Be careful not to put your child in a situation that exceeds his or her capacities or does not offer the support he or she needs to be successful. While high expectations show that you believe in your child, they are likely to place your child in a position to fail rather than succeed without appropriate support. High expectations are beneficial when they align with your child's goals and capacities, and when the support needed to meet them is *willingly provided*.

Many emerging adults continue to benefit from working with a tutor and organizational coach in higher education programs and when taking online or part-time classes. If you want additional help choosing the best path for your child, a college counselor who has experience working with adolescents with LBLDs can be very helpful.

When considering colleges, partner with your teen in the review process. Work together to take into account the following characteristics:

- Location of the campus relative to your home

- Physical size of the campus

- Size of the student population

- Size of the average class

- Access to professors and teaching assistants

- Majors offered

- Philosophy toward special education

- Campus safety

- Campus social life

- Quality of academic support and accommodations

- Quality of social and emotional support services

- Quality of career services

- Access to internships

Transitioning to College and Other Programs

For teens with LBLDs, the transition to college or any postsecondary program is often overwhelming. There are many new academic, social, and emotional demands. In high school, your child generally had your support and that of school personnel and clinicians. In college and other programs, however, this support suddenly decreases or even disappears. Without proper support, many of these emerging adults can flounder.

A Team Approach to Support

Taking a team approach to planning and transitioning will increase your child's chances for a smooth transition into life after high school. The team should comprise you, your child, school personnel, psychologists, life skill coaches, and any other adults who have contributed to your teen's success in high school. Under the direction of you or a designated leader, the team should discuss your child's strengths and needs in all aspects of life. By working together, you can craft a comprehensive and individualized *transition plan*.

Transition plans should take into account each area where support is needed and then establish specific, concrete ways to provide that support. Generally speaking, you want to consider an emerging adult's capacities in the areas of executive functioning skills, academic skills, interpersonal skills, and life skills, including health and well-being. It is essential that all team members agree about what support will be offered and the manner in which it will be provided. Some emerging adults may require high levels of academic support and daily coaching to be successful; others might only need support in one or two areas.

Here are the areas that might benefit from team support:

- Identifying suitable living and eating arrangements

- Maintaining healthy habits

- Establishing a daily routine

- Building meaningful social relationships

- Balancing academics and social life

- Handling academic and interpersonal stress

- Managing competing responsibilities and deadlines

- Developing effective study skills

- Learning to self-advocate

- Problem-solving when faced with obstacles

- Identifying sources of support and counseling

Dealing with Setbacks

No matter how well you and your team plan for the challenges your child will encounter, he or she will inevitably experience a few setbacks. It is important not to view these setbacks as weaknesses. In the face of a crisis, an emerging adult's confidence is fragile. The best response is to help him or her process the situation and provide a context for why it may have occurred. If you are working with a transition team, all can participate in this process, restoring a sense of calm in your child and belief in your collective ability to achieve a solution. This approach will help your child learn from the experience and develop resilience. By anticipating areas of need with a transition plan *and* mindfully addressing setbacks, you will increase the likelihood of a smooth transition not only into college but also into adulthood.

Alternatives to College

Entering college directly after high school is not the best path for *every* emerging adult. Some emerging adults benefit from the opportunity to explore their interests and develop skills outside of a college setting. Here are some meaningful options to consider.

Continued High School Education

As long as your child has an IEP and has not received a high school diploma, he or she is entitled to a public education until the age of twenty-one. Some school districts provide vocational programs for students who opt to stay in school.

Another option is to attend a fifth year of high school at a boarding school. If you are interested in pursuing this path with your teen, carefully do your research—the choices vary enormously and change frequently. It can be a good idea to work with a school placement specialist experienced in this area.

Taking a Gap Year

Among the benefits of a gap year are the extra months of maturation it offers. It also gives emerging adults an opportunity to explore an interest or passion. Some students enter formal gap year programs that involve travel, coursework, and community activities. These programs may be quite expensive, but they usually include room, board, travel, and tuition. Other gap year options include paid and unpaid internships, jobs, and volunteering. While taking a gap year of this type, your child can live at home or on his or her own.

Part-Time or Full-Time Work

Pursuing part- or full-time work after high school can be a productive course of action if carefully planned. There are a number of jobs available to high school graduates that can lead to high-paying and deeply fulfilling careers, such as artisan, chef, technician, salesperson, marketer, and computer programmer.

You can help your child transition into full-time work after high school by finding ways to allow him or her to explore job opportunities while still in high school, especially during the summer months. In some instances, especially if your child has significant LBLDs, you may need to provide him or her with a high level of support in terms of investigating opportunities, completing applications, and working with the prospective employer to secure appropriate accommodations. Increasingly, many employers are eager to embrace diversity in their communities and hire emerging adults who need opportunities to gain skills through working.

Local, state, and federal organizations may be able to help your child transition into jobs. These organizations provide job coaches, mentors, and advocates who help emerging adults identify job opportunities, navigate the application process, and succeed while working. Carefully vet any agency before drawing on its services.

Independent Living

For a variety of reasons (economic and otherwise), in recent decades, the number of emerging adults who live with their parents has increased. The decision to move out is one that requires a healthy, constructive conversation between parent and child. It is important to determine whether the decision is yours or your child's. If it is your decision, carefully consider your motives. Is it that you simply want some separation, or do you feel it is essential for your child's ability to ultimately achieve independence? If it is your child's decision, consider whether independent living will contribute to a healthy quality of life or diminish your child's health and safety.

Here are five key factors to consider when determining whether it is productive for your child to move out of the home and live independently or semi-independently:

Is this a financially viable option?

Does your child have all the skills necessary to successfully manage his or her own living environment?

Is the environment into which your child is intending to move safe and free of negative influences?

Would your child feel emotionally safe and secure in your absence?

If independent living does not work well, would you be willing to have your child move back home?

It is rarely the case that you will answer yes to all five questions, but that does not mean your child shouldn't live independently. When the time comes for your child to live independently, consider working with a professional who can help you and your child evaluate his or her executive functioning skills, interpersonal skills, life skills, and vocational aptitude in order to determine readiness for independent living. As we discussed earlier, developing a plan for moving out of the home and for dealing with any setbacks that arise will be the key to your child's success living independently.

Conclusion

In the final years of high school, you and your teen will begin to recognize that important changes are occurring in all areas of his or her life. With these changes come increased demands, many of which exceed the capacities of emerging adults with LBLDs. Our society encourages young adults to face their challenges independently, but young adults with LBLDs frequently require additional help.

Your ongoing support will be needed to ensure your child's health and well-being as he or she transitions into adulthood. If you discover you need help providing the support your child needs, assemble a team to collaborate with you and your child. Working together, this team can anticipate challenges, provide support, and overcome setbacks.

Work closely with your child to help normalize the support he or she needs while transitioning into life after high school. Achieving independence might take longer and require more effort than either you or your child may have expected, but it will be achieved. A supportive, collaborative approach that embraces a growth mindset and realistic timelines will help your child navigate this stage of his or her life. Continue to trust your heart and instincts while providing the support your child needs. *This is the kinder way.*

Acknowledgments

This book is the outcome of my thirty years working in education. I am first and foremost grateful to my students. The most important lessons I have learned, I have learned from them. These students and their parents inspire me to think deeply about what we can do to make learning a positive experience for everyone—students, parents, and educators.

Over the years, I have had the privilege of collaborating with some of the very best clinicians. Their input allowed me to better serve the students and families in our respective practices and helped shape many of the strategies I share in this book.

I am grateful to the many authors and researchers whose remarkable work and insights I draw on frequently. The areas in which they are recognized below do not reflect the full scope of their work or their influence on me. I apologize for any significant omissions I am likely to have made.

In the areas of reading and dyslexia, I draw on the work of Mary Beth Curtis, Stanislas Dehaene, Susan Hall, Louisa Moats, Hollis Scarborough, Bennett Shaywitz, Sally Shaywitz, Linda Siegel, Margaret Snowling, Joseph Torgesen, and Maryanne Wolf.

In the areas of ADHD and executive functioning, I draw on the work of Russell Barkley, Thomas Brown, Joyce Cooper-Kahn, Laurie Dietzel, Edward Hallowell, Stephen Hinshaw, Martin Kutscher, George McCloskey, Lynn Meltzer, John Ratey, Richard Scheffler, and Larry Silver.

In the areas of motivation, mindset, and instructional practices, I draw on the work of Sian Beilock, Robert Brooks, Carol Dweck, Richard Lavoie, Robert Pianta, Daniel Pink, and Judy Willis.

In the areas of learning and development, I draw on the work of David Cole, Martha Denckla, Donald Deshler, Jack Fletcher, Steven

Forness, Ronald Gallimore, Howard Gardner, Jane Holmes Bernstein, Steve Joordens, Jeanette Norden, Monisha Pasupathi, Jonathan Mooney, Barbara Oakley, Barbara Probst, David Rose, Robert Sapolsky, Roland Tharp, and Deborah Waber.

In the area of parenting, I draw on the work of Sandra Aamodt, Po Bronson, Tina Payne Bryson, Joan Declaire, Sam Goldstein, John Gottman, Mary Hartzell, Ashley Merryman, Gabor Maté, Judith Warner, and Sam Wang.

In the area of interpersonal neurobiology, I draw on the work of Jonathan Baylin, Leslie Brothers, Kurt Fischer, Diana Fosha, Daniel Hughes, Mary Helen Immordino-Yang, Connie Lillas, Kirke Olson, Joseph Palumbo, Stephen Porges, Allan Schore, Daniel Siegel, Marion Solomon, Edward Tronick, and Janiece Turnbull.

I am especially grateful to my dear friend, Louis Cozolino, not only for his remarkable body of work in the area of interpersonal neurobiology but also for his support in the writing of this book.

Many great minds from the past also shaped my thinking and are reflected in this book, including Lev Vygotsky and Jeanne Chall, my mentor while teaching at the Harvard Reading Lab.

I want to thank everyone at the Landmark School in Beverly, Massachusetts. I was lucky to have been a part of this wonderful community as a student and as a teacher.

I also want to thank Dorothy Ungerleider, founder of the Association of Educational Therapists, for her mentorship and direction. It was with Dorothy's encouragement that I was able to start my educational therapy practice and ultimately my educational services company.

In helping me put my thoughts to paper, no two people were more instrumental than my colleagues Jessie Wiener and Rachel Fisher. Jessie tirelessly read my work and provided me with feedback and suggestions. I relied on Rachel's sage-like advice about parenting school-age children and presenting my ideas. I sought advice from Jessie and Rachel at every turn. Without them, this book would never have been written.

I want to thank my extraordinary colleagues Rebecca Borough, Eric Bumatay, Frank Freeman, Ellen Hoffman, Lena Liu, Dominique Marinello, Mojdeh Massachi, Kaitlin McLaughlin, John Posatko, Keri Sills-Payne, Colleen Walsh, and David Walsh for their ideas, support, and encouragement. I was also fortunate to have had the guidance of Elizabeth Heinz, Susan Rabiner, and Charlotte Sheedy.

Ryan Buresh, my editor at New Harbinger Press, has been an integral, patient guide in the development and completion of this book. I would like thank everyone at New Harbinger Press, including Caleb Beckwith, Clancy Drake, Vicraj Gill, Georgia Kolias, and especially Marisa Solís.

I am indebted to my close friends and longtime colleagues Richard Goldman and Peter Murphy for their support and guidance in writing this book. I was also supported by my dear friends and colleagues Nancy Anderson, Alden Denny Blodget, Amanda Datnow, Scott Harris, Don Sloggy, Michael Spagna, and Nicholas Thaler. In particular, I want to thank Crystal I. Lee for her collaboration on our chapter on young adults.

My childhood friend Keith Meldahl, an accomplished author in his own right, was especially helpful throughout the entire process. Virginia Jane (VJ) Nelson, my high school librarian, has always been a source of great support and friendship. My heartfelt thanks also go to Barbara Baker, Rick Calomino, Ellen Curtis, Daniel Dejean, Genevieve Mathis, Julia Murphy, Mary Oliver, and Anthony Sherin.

It is with deep appreciation that I recognize my former teachers Mrs. Shirley Gott and Mrs. Eleanor Meldahl. These two extraordinary educators helped me prevail and inspired a career choice that rewards me every day.

I am incredibly grateful to my siblings, Maria, Ben, and Josh, and their families, for their consistent encouragement and support. I am especially grateful to my mother and my father, Rachel and Graham, who gave me the one thing any child ever really needs: unconditional love.

Further Reading

Barkley, R. 2005. *ADHD and The Nature of Self-Control*. New York: Guilford Press.

Baylin, J., and D. A. Hughes. 2016. *The Neurobiology of Attachment-Focused Therapy*. New York: W.W. Norton & Company.

Bernstein, J., K. W. Fischer, and M. H. Immordino-Yang, eds. 2012. *Mind, Brain, and Education in Reading Disorders*. Cambridge: Cambridge University Press.

Bronson, P., and A. Merryman. 2009. *NurtureShock: New Thinking About Children*. New York: Twelve.

Brooks, R., and S. Goldstein. 2003. *The Power of Resilience: Achieving Balance, Confidence, and Personal Strength in Your Life*. New York: McGraw-Hill.

Chall, J. S. 1983. *Stages of Reading Development*. New York: McGraw-Hill.

Cooper-Kahn, J., and L. Dietzel. 2008. *Late, Lost, and Unprepared: A Parents' Guide to Helping Children with Executive Functioning*. Bethesda, MD: Woodbine House.

Cozolino, L. 2014. *The Neuroscience of Human Relationships: Attachment and the Developing Social Brain*. New York: W.W. Norton & Company.

Curtis, M. B. 1999. *When Adolescents Can't Read: Methods and Materials That Work*. Northampton, MA: Brookline.

Dehaene, S. 2009. *Reading in the Brain: The New Science of How We Read*. New York: Penguin.

Gardner, H. 2011. *The Unschooled Mind: How Children Think and How Schools Should Teach.* New York City: Basic Books.

Goleman, D. 2005. *Emotional Intelligence: Why It Can Matter More Than IQ.* New York: Bantam.

Gottman, J., and J. DeClaire. 1998. *Raising an Emotionally Intelligent Child: The Heart of Parenting.* New York: Simon & Schuster.

Greene, R. W. 2001. *The Explosive Child: A New Approach for Understanding and Parenting Easily Frustrated, Chronically Inflexible Children.* New York: Quill Press.

Greene, R. W. 2008. *Lost at School: Why Our Kids with Behavioral Challenges Are Falling Through the Cracks and How We Can Help Them.* New York: Scribner.

Fonagy, P., M. Target, D. Cottrell, J. Phillips, and Z. Kurtz. 2005. *What Works for Whom: A Critical Review of Treatments for Children and Adolescents.* New York: The Guilford Press.

Fox, J. 2009. *Your Child's Strengths: A Guide for Parents and Teachers.* New York: Penguin Books.

Hall, S. L., and L. C. Moats. 2002. *Parenting a Struggling Reader.* New York: Broadway Books.

Hallowell, E. M. and J. J. Ratey. 1994. *Driven to Distraction: Recognizing and Coping with Attention Deficit Disorder from Childhood Through Adulthood.* New York: Touchstone Books.

Harris, A. J., and E. R. Sipay. 1985. *How to Increase Reading Ability: A Guide to Developmental and Remedial Methods,* eighth edition. New York: Longman.

Hinshaw, S., and R. Scheffler. 2014. *The ADHD Explosion: Myths, Medication, Money, and Today's Push for Performance.* Oxford, UK: Oxford University Press.

Hutton, J., T. Horowitz-Kraus, A. Mendelsohn, T. DeWitt, and S. Holland. 2015. "Home Reading Environment and Brain Activation in Preschool Children Listening to Stories." *Pediatrics* 136 (3, August

10): 466–78. http://pediatrics.aappublications.org/content/pediatrics/136/3/466.full.pdf.

Kavale, K. A., and S. R. Forness. 1995. *The Nature of Learning Disabilities: Critical Elements of Diagnosis and Classification*. Abingdon, UK: Routledge.

Kutscher, M. L. 2009. *ADHD: Living Without Brakes*. London, UK: Jessica Kingsley Publishers.

Lillas, C., and J. Turnbull. 2009. *Infant/Child Mental Health, Early Intervention, and Relationship-Based Techniques: A Neurorelational Framework for Interdisciplinary Practice*. New York: W.W. Norton & Company.

Maté, G. 2000. *Scattered: How Attention Deficit Disorder Originates and What You Can Do About It*. New York: Plume.

McCloskey, G., L. A. Perkins, and B. C. Divner. 2009. *Assessment and Intervention for Executive Function Difficulties*. New York: Routledge.

Meltzer, L., 2007. *Executive Function in Education*. New York: The Guilford Press.

Mooney, J., and D. Cole. 2000. *Learning Outside the Lines: Two Ivy League Students with Learning Disabilities and ADHD Give You the Tools for Academic Success and Educational Revolution*. New York: Fireside.

Newhall, P. W. 2012. *Language-Based Learning Disabilities*. Prides Crossing, MA: Landmark School Outreach Program.

Neufeld, G., and G. Maté. 2006. *Hold On to Your Kids: Why Parents Need to Matter More Than Peers*. New York: Ballantine Books.

Oakley, B. 2014. *A Mind for Numbers: How to Excel at Math and Science (Even If You Flunked Algebra)*. New York: Tarcher/Penguin.

Olson, K. 2014. *The Invisible Classroom: Relationships, Neuroscience & Mindfulness in School*. New York: W.W. Norton & Company.

Palombo, J. 2001. *Learning Disorders & Disorders of the Self in Children and Adolescents*. New York: W.W. Norton & Company.

Pasupathi, M., and K. McLean. 2010. *Silence and Memory: A Special Issue on Memory.* Hove, East Sussex: Psychology Press.

Prizant, B. M. 2015. *Uniquely Human: A Different Way of Seeing Autism.* New York: Simon and Schuster.

Probst, B. 2008. *When the Labels Don't Fit: A New Approach to Raising a Challenging Child.* New York: Three Rivers Press.

Putnam, L. R. 1997. *Readings on Language and Literacy: Essays in Honor of Jeanne S. Chall.* Cambridge, MA: Brookline Books.

Rath, T. 2007. *StrengthsFinder 2.0.* Washington, DC: Gallup Press.

Schiltz, K., A. Schonfeld, and T. Niendam. 2011. *Beyond the Label: A Guide to Unlocking a Child's Educational Potential.* Oxford, UK: Oxford University Press.

Seligman, M. E. P. 2006. *Learned Optimism: How to Change Your Mind and Your Life,* second edition. New York: Vintage Books.

Siegel, D. J. 1999. *The Developing Mind: How Relationships and the Brain Interact to Shape Who We Are.* New York: The Guilford Press.

Siegel, D. J. 2007. *The Mindful Brain: Reflection and Attunement in the Cultivation of Well-Being.* New York: W.W. Norton & Company.

Siegel, D. J., and M. Solomon. 2017. *How People Change: Relationships and Neuroplasticity in Psychotherapy.* New York: W.W. Norton & Company.

Siegel, D. J., and T. P. Bryson. 2011. *The Whole-Brain Child: 12 Revolutionary Strategies to Nurture Your Child's Developing Mind.* New York: Delacourte Press.

Silver, L. B. 1984. *The Misunderstood Child: A Guide for Parents of Learning Disabled Children.* New York: McGraw-Hill.

Silver, L. B. 1999. *Dr. Larry Silver's Advice to Parents on Attention Deficit Hyperactivity Disorder.* New York: Times Books.

Snowling, M. 1990. *Dyslexia: A Cognitive Developmental Perspective.* Cambridge, MA: Basil Blackwell.

Stewart, K. 2007. *Helping a Child with Nonverbal Learning Disorder or Asperger's Disorder*, second edition. Oakland, CA: New Harbinger Publications, Inc.

Thaler, N. 2016. *The Parent's Guide to Neuropsychology.* Printed by CreateSpace.

Tharp, R. G., and R. Gallimore. 1988. *Rousing Minds to Life: Teaching, Learning, and Schooling in Social Context.* New York: Cambridge University Press.

Tough, P. 2012. *How Children Succeed: Grit, Curiosity, and the Hidden Power of Character.* New York: Houghton Mifflin Harcourt.

Ungerleider, D. 1998. *Reading, Writing, and Rage: The Terrible Price Paid by Victims of School Failure.* Encino, CA: RWR Press.

Vygotsky, L. 1992. *Thought and Language.* Edited by A. Kozulin. Cambridge, MA: The MIT Press.

Vygotsky, L. S. 1978. *Mind in Society: The Development of Higher Psychological Processes.* Edited by M. Cole, V. John-Steiner, S. Scribner, and E. Souberman. Cambridge, MA: Harvard University Press.

Waber, D. P. 2010. *Rethinking Learning Disabilities: Understanding Children who Struggle in School.* New York: The Guilford Press.

Warner, J. 2010. *We've Got Issues: Children and Parents in the Age of Medication.* New York: Riverhead Books.

Willis, J. 2009. *How Your Child Learns Best: Brain-Friendly Strategies You Can Use to Ignite Your Child's Learning and Increase School Success.* Naperville, IL: Source Books.

Wolf, M. 2008. *Proust and the Squid: The Story and Science of the Reading Brain.* New York: Harper Perennial.

References

Aamodt, S., and S. Wang. 2011. *Welcome to Your Child's Brain*. New York: Bloomsbury USA.

Arnett, J. 2014. *Emerging Adulthood: The Winding Road from the Late Teens Through the Twenties*. New York: Oxford University Press.

Beilock, S. 2011. *Choke: What the Secrets of the Brain Reveal About Getting It Right When You Have To*. New York: Atria Books.

Brooks, R., and S. Goldstein. 2001. *Raising Resilient Children: Fostering Strength, Hope, and Optimism in Your Child*. Chicago: Contemporary Books.

Brown, T. E. 2005. *Attention Deficit Disorder: The Unfocused Mind in Children and Adults*. New Haven, CT: Yale University Press.

Carr, P. B., and G. Walton. 2014. "Cues of Working Together Fuel Intrinsic Motivation and Can Contribute to the Solution of Collective Action Problems." *Journal of Experimental Social Psychology* 53: 169–84.

Cozolino, L. 2013. *The Social Neuroscience of Education: Optimizing Attachment & Learning in the Classroom*. New York: W.W. Norton & Company.

Denckla, M. 2013. "Most Learning Disabilities are Language Based: Remembering the Spoken Language Foundation of the 3's." McLean School of Maryland video, 1:10:21, January 15. https://www.youtube.com/watch?v=GE16nduqKgs&t=23s.

Dweck, C. S. 2007. *Mindset: The New Psychology of Success*. New York: Ballantine Books.

Ficksman, M., and J. U. Adelizzi, eds. 2010. *The Clinical Practice of Educational Therapy: A Teaching Model.* New York: Routledge.

Fletcher J. M., G. R. Lyon, L. S. Fuchs, and M. A. Barnes. 2006. *Learning Disabilities: From Identification to Intervention.* New York: The Guilford Press.

Forbes, H., and B. Post. 2009. *Beyond Consequences, Logic, and Control: A Love-Based Approach to Helping Children with Severe Behaviors.* Boulder, CO: Beyond Consequences Institute.

Fuligni, A. J., and C. Hardway. 2006. "Daily Variation in Adolescents' Sleep, Activities, and Psychological Well-Being." *Journal of Research on Adolescence* 16 (3): 353–78.

Hershner, S., and R. Chervin. 2014. "Causes and Consequences of Sleepiness Among College Students." *Nature and Science of Sleep* Volume b: 73–84.

Hughes, D. A. 2009. *Attachment-Focused Parenting: Effective Strategies to Care for Children.* New York: W.W. Norton & Company.

Immordino-Yang, M. H. 2016. *Emotions, Learning, and the Brain: Exploring the Educational Implications of Affective Neuroscience.* New York: W.W. Norton & Company.

Individuals with Disabilities Education Act (IDEA). 2004. 20 U.S.C. § 1400.

Individuals with Disabilities Education Act (IDEA). 2012. 34 CFR § 300.8.

Jimerson, S. R. 2001. "Meta-Analysis of Grade Retention Research: Implications for Practice in the 21st Century." *School Psychology Review* 30: 420–37.

Kohn, A. 1999. *Punished by Rewards: The Trouble with Gold Stars, Incentive Plans, A's, Praises, and Other Bribes.* Boston, MA: Houghton Mifflin Harcourt.

Lavoie, R. 2007. *The Motivation Breakthrough: 6 Secrets to Turning on the Tuned-Out Child.* New York: Touchstone Books.

Lutz, A., L. Greischar, N. Rawlings, M. Ricard, and R. Davidson. 2004. "Long-Term Meditators Self-Induce High-Amplitude Gamma Synchrony During Mental Practice." *Proceedings of the National Academy of Sciences*, November 16. http://www.pnas.org/content /101/46/16369.full.

Melby-Lervåg, M., T. Redick, and C. Hulme. 2016. "Working Memory Training Does Not Improve Performance on Measures of Intelligence or Other Measures of 'Far Transfer': Evidence from a Meta-Analytic Review." *Perspectives on Psychological Science* 11 (4): 512–34.

Meyer, A. D., D. H. Rose, and D. T. Gordon. 2014. *Universal Design for Learning: Theory and Practice*. Wakefield, MA: CAST Professional Publishing.

Neighmond, P. 2006. "Exercise Helps Students in the Classroom." *Morning Edition*, NPR. August 31.

Panicker, A., and A. Chelliah. 2016. "Resilience and Stress in Children and Adolescents with Specific Learning Disability." *Journal of the Canadian Academy of Child and Adolescent Psychiatry* winter: 17–23. https://www.ncbi.nlm.nih.gov/pmc/articles/PMC4791102/pdf/ccap25 _p0017.pdf.

Pianta, R. 2000. *Enhancing Relationships Between Children and Teachers*. Washington, DC: American Psychological Association.

Pink, D. 2011. *Drive: The Surprising Truth About What Motivates Us*. New York: Riverhead Books.

Rehabilitation Act of 1973. 1973. Section 504, 34 C.F.R.

Rose, T. 2016. *The End of Average: How We Succeed in a World That Values Sameness*. San Francisco, CA: HarperOne.

Sanders, L. 2017. "Flex Time: The Brain's Ability to Shift Connections Might Ease Learning." *Science News* September 16: 22–25.

Sansone, C., D. B. Thoman, and T. Fraughton. 2015. "The Relation Between Interest and Self-Regulation in Mathematics and Science." In K. A. Renninger, M. Neiswandt, and S. Hidi (Eds.) *Interest in*

Mathematics and Science Learning. Washington, DC: American Educational Research Association.

Sapolsky, R. M. 2004. *Why Zebras Don't Get Ulcers: The Acclaimed Guide to Stress, Stress-Related Diseases, and Coping,* third edition. New York: St. Martin's Griffin.

Shaywitz, S. 2005. *Overcoming Dyslexia: A New and Complete Science-Based Program for Reading Problems at Any Level.* New York: Vintage Books.

Siegel, D. J., and M. Hartzell. 2013. *Parenting from the Inside Out: How a Deeper Self-Understanding Can Help You Raise Children Who Thrive.* Brunswick, Victoria, Australia: Scribe Publications.

Stanovich, K. 1986. "Matthew Effects in Reading: Some Consequences of Individual Differences in the Acquisition of Literacy." *Reading Research Quarterly* fall: 360–407.

Daniel Franklin, PhD, holds a master's degree from the Harvard Graduate School of Education in reading, language, and learning disabilities, as well as a PhD in education from the University of California, Los Angeles. He has over thirty years of experience in education as a teacher, administrator, and consultant. Franklin is founder and president of Los Angeles, CA-based Franklin Educational Services, Inc., which provides individualized school support services for students of all ages and needs.

Foreword writer Louis Cozolino, PhD, is professor of psychology at Pepperdine University Graduate School of Education and Psychology, and author of *The Social Neuroscience of Education.*

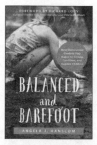

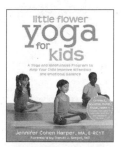

Register your **new harbinger** titles for additional benefits!

When you register your **new harbinger** title—purchased in any format, from any source—you get access to benefits like the following:

- Downloadable accessories like printable worksheets and extra content

- Instructional videos and audio files

- Information about updates, corrections, and new editions

Not every title has accessories, but we're adding new material all the time.

Access free accessories in 3 easy steps:

1. Sign in at NewHarbinger.com (or **register** to create an account).

2. Click on **register a book**. Search for your title and click the **register** button when it appears.

3. Click on the **book cover or title** to go to its details page. Click on **accessories** to view and access files.

That's all there is to it!

If you need help, visit:

NewHarbinger.com/accessories

new harbinger
CELEBRATING
40 YEARS